To Be Continued.

A 21st Century Update of the Heidelberg Catechism
of the Christian Church from North Central Java

Published by the Synod of the
Christian Church from North Central Java

To Be Continued:

A 21st Century Update of the Heidelberg Catechism of the Christian Church from North Central Java

GKJTU

The Teaching of the GKJTU

On Culture, Religious Plurality
And Denominational Variety,
Politics, Economics
As Well as Arts, Science and Technology

Official English Translation

Published by the Synod of the GKJTU

WIPF & STOCK · Eugene, Oregon

TO BE CONTINUED
A 21st Century Update of the Heidelberg Catechism of the Christian Church from North Central Java

Copyright © 2014 Verlag fur Kultur und Wissenschaft. All rights reserved. Except for brief quotations in critical publications or reviews, no part of this book may be reproduced in any manner without prior written permission from the publisher. Write: Permissions, Wipf and Stock Publishers, 199 W. 8th Ave., Eugene, OR 97401.

This Edition published by Wipf and Stock Publishers in cooperation with Verlag fur Kultur und Wissenschaft.

Wipf & Stock
An imprint of Wipf and Stock Publishers
199 W. 8th Avenue, Suite 3
Eugene OR, 97401
www.wipfandstock.com

ISBN 13: 978-1-4982-0631-0
Manufactured in the U.S.A.

Contents

Contents	5
Detailed Contents	6
Translators' Preface	13
Introduction (by GKJTU)	19
Twenty-First Century Update of the Heidelberg Catechism by the GKJTU	21
A. **Realm of Culture**	**21**
B. **Realm of Religious Plurality and the Diversity of Christian Churches**	**41**
C. **Realm of Politics**	**57**
D. **Realm of Economy**	**71**
E. **Realm of Science and Technology**	**79**
Index	95

Detailed Contents

Contents 5
Detailed Contents 6
Translators' Preface 13
Introduction (by GKJTU) 19
Twenty-First Century Update of the Heidelberg Catechism by the GKJTU 21

   A. Realm of Culture   **21**

    Question 1:   What is the meaning of 'culture'?   21

    Question 2:   What is our attitude towards culture?   22

    Question 3:   How can culture be renewed?   22

    Question 4:   What is the meaning of '*adat*' and '*adat*-ceremonies'?   24

    Question 5:   What is our attitude towards '*adat*-ceremonies'?   24

    Question 6:   According to some people, '*adat*-ceremonies' are useful as a means of gaining wellbeing and getting saved. Can man be saved by God through practicing '*adat* ceremonies'?   25

    Question 7:   '*Adat*-ceremonies' often are closely linked to sorcery, magic, forth telling, interpreting dreams etc. According to the Christian faith, do things like this determine human fate?   26

    Question 8:   What is the attitude of individual Christians and of the church as a whole towards '*adat*-ceremonies' and everything connected with '*adat*', based on the understanding of the term explained above?   27

    Question 9:   One '*adat*-ceremony' connected to the cycle of life is the wedding ceremony. What is the attitude of the Christian faith towards '*adat*-ceremonies' on the occasion of a wedding?   28

    Question 10:   One expression of culture is the realm of marriage, which can vary widely depending on the local culture and various periods of history. What is our view concerning marriage?   29

    Question 11:   Another ceremony connected with the cycle of life is circumcision. What is our view of circumcision?   31

Question 12: In order to promote harmony in society all citizens, including Christians, will be involved in all kinds of social activities, such as communal work, mutual helping among neighbors, funerals, help in natural disasters, activities as a board member of a social organization etc. Are Christians allowed to be diverted by these activities from attending a church service?   32

Question 13: Other expressions of culture are the traditional fine arts, such as *'reog'*, *'wayang'*, *'ludruk'*, *'ketoprak'*, *'campursari'* et al. What is the attitude of GKJTU members towards these expressions of fine arts?   33

Question 14: In the field of musical arts sometimes new lyrics are combined with an already known melody (which is called *kontrafaktur* by the experts). What is our attitude towards this?   35

Question 15: Clothing is also a form of art. What is our view concerning clothing?   36

Question 16: So far we have discussed many issues of Javanese culture. Is the GKJTU indeed a church for the Javanese only?   37

Question 17: Why does the GKJTU esteem high the diversity of culture and language?   38

B. Realm of Religious Plurality and the Diversity of Christian Churches   **41**

Question 18: What is meant by 'plurality' and 'pluralism'?   41

Question 19: The different religions are one form of plurality within Indonesian society. What is actually meant by the term 'religion'? 42

Question 20: What is our view concerning religion?   42

Question 21: According to the Christian faith, where does religious plurality come from?   43

Question 22: What is our attitude towards the plurality of religions?   45

Question 23: During the encounter between different religious communities some take a fanatic attitude by humiliating or even insulting others. One example is to call the adherents of other religions heathens. What is our attitude when we are called heathens?   46

Question 24: In a situation of religious plurality the religious communities spread their respective religion. This can lead to conflicts among the religious communities. How does the church proclaim the Gospel in the midst of this religious plurality? 48

Question 25: How do the Christians work out their relationship with other religious communities? 49

Question 26: A society with religious plurality very easily leads to religious intermarriage. What is our view and attitude concerning this issue? 50

Question 27: It may happen that adherents of different religions meet and pray together for the issues they face together. What is our view and attitude concerning this phenomenon? 52

Question 28: Within Christianity there is also a plurality. What is our attitude when working out our relationship with diverse kinds of Christian movements and denominations? 53

Question 29: To live within a context of church variety makes it possible to attend the meetings of other churches. What is our view and attitude concerning attendance at the meetings of other churches? 55

C. Realm of Politics 57

Question 30: What is the meaning of the term 'politics'? 57

Question 31: What then is the state? 57

Question 32: The state is an organization or institution that exercises power. So what is that state power all about? 58

Question 33: Who exercises this state authority? 58

Question 34: Every government holds and executes authority. Where does this authority originate from? 59

Question 35: Which of these three sources of state authority are according to the Bible? 60

Question 36: Why does the Bible teach that the power of the state has to be received as a grace of God? 60

Question 37: The Bible has the understanding that the power of the state is a gift of God. So what is then the attitude of the Christians towards state and government? 61

Question 38: What conditions have to be fulfilled by a state and a government to be respected and obeyed by the Christians and the other citizens? 62

Question 39: What can Christians as fellow citizens do if the state does not fulfill the above-mentioned conditions? 62

Question 40: What is necessary for the state to fulfill its function properly? 63

Question 41: Why does the law also have to be applied to those in power and why is it necessary to guard and control those in power? 64

Question 42: In what ways do Christians participate in the life of the state? 64

Question 43: Everything explained thus far is about the relationship of the state or politics with the people. So how about the relationship of the church towards the state and towards politics? 66

Question 44: So what does the cooperation of politics / the state and the Church actually look like? 67

Question 45: May the church be active in politics? 68

Question 46: So how about the calling of the Church to proclaim the mandate of Christ in all aspects of life? Is the realm of politics an exception? 69

Question 47: How can the independence and freedom of the church with regard to politics and state affairs be safeguarded? 69

D. Realm of Economy 71

Question 48: What is meant by 'economy' and 'business'? 71

Question 49: Does the Bible also talk about economy and business? 72

Question 50: The Bible indeed talks a lot about economy and business. So what then is the biblical view of economy and business enterprises? 74

Question 51: Basically economy and business are firmly rooted in the mandate of God. Why then do many Christians think that economy and business are dirty endeavors? 74

Question 52: How then do Christians run economy and
business? 75

Question 53: How can we accomplish the plan of God in the
aforementioned realm of economy and business? 76

Question 54: Is the church as an institution allowed to engage in
economic and business activities? 77

Question 55: If the church is thus allowed to engage in economic and business activities, in what kind of activities may the
church be engaged? 78

E. Realm of Science and Technology 79

Question 56: What is the meaning of science and technology? 79

Question 57: Why do humans possess science, humanities and
technology? 80

Question 58: Are science and technology not contrary to human
destiny ('*kodrat*')? 81

Question 59: Does that mean that God has completely surrendered His creation into the hands of mankind? 82

Question 60: Why can science and technology also be used to
damage God's creation? 83

Question 61: Thus science and technology can become both a
blessing and a curse. Which examples can be cited for this? 84

Question 62: One very obvious and perceptible negative effect
of science and technology is the destruction of the environment. How do science and technology destroy the environment? 85

Question 63: What are the effects of this destruction of the
environment for human life and for life in general? 87

Question 64: The sin of man influences science and technology
in a special form in Indonesia. What is that special form? 87

Question 65: Can science, humanities and technology help
mankind to return to God? 88

Question 66: Does salvation in Christ also affect science,
humanities and technology? 89

Detailed Contents

Question 67: How can believers discern between the blessings and the disastrous aspects of science, humanities and technology?   90

Question 68: What is our attitude, if the results of science and humanities are contrary to the teachings of the Bible?   91

Question 69: What is the role of the church, when faith is applied in the field of science, humanities and technology?   92

Index   95

Translators' Preface

Since becoming independent many churches in Asia, Africa and Latin America have formulated their own creeds, replacing the traditional creeds they inherited from European Churches. Those new creeds were intended to reformulate Christian faith facing new challenges. Just some examples from Indonesia: When the Batak Church HKBP became a member of the Lutheran World Federation they would not sign the Augsburg Confession as was customary for LWF member churches before. Instead they proposed their own creed, the 'Konfesi HKBP' which had been endorsed by HKBP in 1951. In a similar way the reformed Javanese Christian Church ('*Gereja-gereja Kristen Jawa*' – GKJ) endorsed the *Points of Teaching of the Javanese Christian Church* (*Pokok-pokok Ajaran GKJ*) in 1996, to replace the Heidelberg Catechism which had until than been used in the GKJ.

The reformed 'Karo-Batak-Church' in North Sumatra formulated their own creed in 1979, the reformed 'Toraja-Church' in Sulawesi endorsed theirs in 1981 and the 'Communion of Churches in Indonesia' (*Persekutuan Gereja-gereja Indonesia* – PGI) received a common creed in 1984, although these latter three were not necessarily meant to replace the Heidelberg Catechism. (For an English translation of the three see *Reformed Witness Today,* ed. Lukas Vischer, Bern, 1982, pp. 31-58).

The 'Christian Church from North Central Java' (*Gereja Kristen Jawa Tengah Utara* – GKJTU) has deliberately chosen its own special way: The GKJTU further on acknowledges the Heidelberg Catechism of 1563 as the binding summary of the Holy Scriptures and a universal creed uniting reformational churches all over the world and through the ages. Only for specific questions of its Javanese context (culture, religious pluralism) and modern challenges (politics, economics, science and technology) has the GKJTU supplemented and updated the Heidelberg Catechism.

The connection of this Twenty-First Century Update of the Heidelberg Catechism is visible by its outward structure: Question – Answer – Scripture citations (notwithstanding the fact that in the GKJTU update the questions are often introduced by a sentence connecting it with the previous questions). But also the cross references to the Heidelberg Catechism connects the two documents, as well as the common theological structure of fall and redemption.

But the decision of the GKJTU is also remarkable from a second standpoint: Actually the GKJTU originated from the work of an interdenominational faith mission, i.e. the 'Salatiga Mission' / 'Neukirchener Mission'. These interdenominational mission agencies had deliberately not forced any Lutheran, Reformed, Baptist or other denominational creed onto the newly founded congregations. Thus GKJTU at its 23rd Synod Assembly in 1988 was completely free to choose the Heidelberg Catechism as their creed. At its 27th Synod Assembly in 2008 the GKJTU added the update presented here. Thereby the GKJTU has found its identity as a 'Calvinist-pietistic-contextual' or in simple terms: 'reformational church' (a formula coined by the 26th Synod Assembly in 2003). Most likely it was because the GKJTU had freely and deliberately chosen this Calvinist-pietistic-contextual identity (including the Heidelberg Catechism and its update), that GKJTU has a much more positive attitude towards these traditions compared to many other Indonesian churches.

In general the members of the GKJTU have a very positive attitude towards their church, which therefore is often called 'the beloved GKJTU'. That is why the catechism update alternately and almost interchangeably talks about 'Christians', 'the GKJTU' or just uses the pronoun 'we'.

Modern creeds always struggle to give answers to contemporary issues, and therefore they have to be revised from time to time. In 1996 the Batak Church HKBP thoroughly revised their aforementioned confession from 1951.The *Points of Teaching of the Javanese Christian Church* from 1996 were already slightly revised in 2005. Also the common creed of the Communion of Churches in Indonesia (PGI) of 1984 has been complemented several times since then. Accordingly the GKJTU is open to revision (or further updates) of their catechism update of 2008. But concerning the Heidelberg Catechism itself the GKJTU states (in contrast to the views of many other Asian theologians): "... the *Heidelberg Catechism* itself comprises the basic teaching for the reformational churches throughout the ages." (Compare below, *Introduction by GKJTU*, p. 19).

One of the characteristics of the Heidelberg Catechism are the scripture proofs diligently provided for every one of its answers. In its first edition in 1563 these Bible verses were just named, but not written out. Thus the reader was guided to open and read those verses in their biblical context. But it was not certain whether the reader would really open these scripture passages, so in many later editions the Scripture references were written out. This is common practice in most Indonesian editions of the Heidelberg Catechism, and the GKJTU Update follows that tradition. When the verse is quoted in full it also clarifies which translation (and interpretation) of the verse the argumentation is based on.

Translator's Preface

The full, original title of the Heidelberg Catechism was: „Catechismus Oder Christlicher Vnderricht, wie der in Kirchen vnd Schulen der Churfürstlichen Pfaltz getrieben wirdt" ("Catechism or Christian Teaching as taught in the Churches and Schools of the Electoral Palatinate"), which has then been modified by reformed churches in several countries. Accordingly the Indonesian edition of the Heidelberg Catechism has for a long time borne the title *Christian Teaching – the Heidelberg Catechism (Pengajaran Agama Kristen – Katekismus Heidelberg).* This explains also the title of the GKJTU-Update: *A 21st Century Update of the Heidelberg Catechism – The Teaching of the GKJTU On Culture, Religious Plurality And Denominational Variety, Politics, Economics As Well As On Science, Arts And Technology.* Thus the GKJTU uses the similarity of the Indonesian words '*ajaran*' (teaching, doctrine) and '*pengajaran*' (instruction, teaching). By choosing this title the GKJTU wants to stress firstly that this Update is of course meant for the members of the GKJTU only, whereas the Heidelberg Catechism is meant for all Christians all over the world. Secondly the Heidelberg Catechism comprises the basis for the whole of Christian doctrine, whereas the Update of the GKJTU is restricted to the aforementioned realms.

The Heidelberg Catechism has been used by Indonesian churches mainly for catechism classes preceding baptism and for confirmation classes, which therefore are called '*katekisasi*' in Indonesian. Whereas a regular lecture of the Catechism as part of the liturgy let alone sermons on the Catechism – as it is a rule in many reformed churches – has been more or less unknown in the GKJTU. Therefore it has to be stressed in the introduction to the Update: "These two books of doctrine of the GKJTU (The *Heidelberg Catechism* and its *Update*) should be used not only for catechism classes and confirmation classes, but also on other occasions, e.g. being cited in sermons, read as a part of the liturgy, ..." (Compare below, *Introduction by GKJTU*, p. 19).

The (partly necessarily quite dynamic) translation presented here is an attempt to make this GKJTU-Update of the Heidelberg Catechism accessible for interested readers without demanding special knowledge in theology, Indonesian language or Javanese culture. It is also intended for readers who speak English not as their mother tongue, but only as a second (or may be even as a third or fourth) language. Therefore an over-exact expert terminology was avoided. Notes were added which provide background information for readers not acquainted with Javanese culture.

In this translation the English scripture citations are taken from the *New Revised Standard Version* (1989) if not otherwise stated. Other translations are cited if their wording is closer to the wording of the official Indonesian Bible

Society Translation ('*Terjemahan Baru*') cited in the original GKJTU-Update of the Heidelberg Catechism and thus make its understanding easier. In three cases (Mt 19:6, question no. 9; 1Cor 5:12-13, question no. 22; Job 37:23, question 65) the translators even had to provide their own translation of the verse, because no English translation could be found which really reflected the understanding of the Bible text as in the official Indonesian translation of those verses.

In many instances the answers of the GKJTU-Update might seem strangely ambiguous to the European reader (and may be even stranger for the American reader, who might prefer more practical answers). This ambiguity is caused firstly by the deliberate shortness of the catechism update, which makes it impossible to give a more detailed answer. Secondly the GKJTU stresses the reformational freedom, which cannot accept casuistic and legalistic answers. Thirdly in many particular questions the congregations of the GKJTU have not yet come to a common attitude, just this Update shall cautiously help the congregations to get to such a common stance. Fourthly the Javanese readers find it much easier to apply these general types of advice to their day to day life; only the reader who is not so well-acquainted with Javanese culture might wonder what the proposed action might look like. Finally it is a feature of Javanese culture not to give directive answers but to allow a bit of mystery to remain. These facts are expressed by a common saying among Javanese Christians: If you ask a charismatic Pentecostal preacher concerning a given issue, he will answer with a clear 'Yes' or 'No'. But if you ask a reformational (Javanese) pastor, he surely would answer: 'Yes, but ...'

Nevertheless this translation in its annotations tries to supply examples from the life of the GKJTU, which might help to make the answers of the GKJTU-Update more understandable.

It has to be kept in mind, too, that the GKJTU-Update has been worked out by a team with several sub teams and several revisions. Although the final redactor tried to produce a homogenous text, the depths and the way of argumentation are still a bit different in various parts of the Update. The GKJTU deliberately put up with this heterogeneity, instead of forcing a fully consistent text from one single theological 'genius' onto the congregations.

On this occasion the GKJTU also thanks Dr. Helen Miehle and all other friends of the GKJTU who contributed a lot of valuable critical remarks to this English translation.

This present translation together with its annotations has been accepted by the Moderamen / Board of the GKJTU. Therefore it is the official English

Translator's Preface

translation of the *Twenty-First Century Update of the Heidelberg Catechism by the Christian Church from North Central Java.*

It is our hope that by the translation provided here the GKJTU-Update to the Heidelberg Catechism will become an inspiration and a blessing also for many people outside Java.

The translators

Rev. Dr. Christian Goßweiler &
Kristanti Pebri Nugrahani Goßweiler

Introduction (by GKJTU)

The Church of the Lord is called to grow, to blossom and to bring forth fruit. Nevertheless the members of the Christian Church from North Central Java (*Gereja Kristen Jawa Tengah Utara* – GKJTU) face many problems and struggles in their day-to-day life, which often are not completely answered. Thus their day-to-day problems do not diminish but increase. To overcome these problems the members of the GKJTU need a firm belief, a clear confession of faith and a clear Christian moral stance. In order for this belief to be strengthened, the members of the GKJTU need clear teaching about the basics of Christian faith so that they can overcome these problems in the right way.

The GKJTU is well aware that many of these problems are caused by deep and wholesome changes in the realm of culture, in the realm of religious plurality and denominational variety, in the realm of politics, in the realm of economics as well as in the realm of science, arts and technology. As a church we are called to take a clear stance in all these fields.

To be faithful to this calling, the GKJTU is publishing this booklet, the *Twenty-First Century Update of the Heidelberg Catechism by the Christian Church from North Central Java. – The Teaching of the GKJTU On Culture, Religious Plurality And Denominational Variety, Politics, Economy As Well As Science, Arts And Technology*. This booklet was a mandate of the 26th General Synod Assembly of the GKJTU in 2003.[1] Several experts from inside and outside the GKJTU together with the congregations of the GKJTU have worked together to design this booklet, under the coordination by the formation institute LPPPK GKJTU '*Sabda Mulya*' (LPPPK GKJTU = '*Lembaga Pendidikan, Pembinaan dan Pengaderan Kristen Gereja Kristen Jawa Tengah Utara*' = 'Institute for Christian Education, Formation and Forming of Cadres of the Christian Church from North Central Java'). A survey was used to collect the ideas and questions of the congregations and this input was further processed through the meetings of a workgroup and through a workshop. Finally the 27th General Synod Assembly in October 2008 was able to officially accept this Update of the Heidelberg Catechism as a handbook and update to the book *Christian Teaching – The Heidelberg Catechism*.[2]

---

[1] *Official Report of the 26th General Synod Assembly of the GKJTU*, art. 51.2.
[2] *Official Report of the 27th General Synod Assembly of the GKJTU*, art. 36-38.

Because of its nature as an update, this *Twenty-First Century Update of the Heidelberg Catechism* is really meant only as an addition to the *Heidelberg Catechism*, not to replace it. For the GKJTU the *Heidelberg Catechism* is still the summary of the Holy Scriptures and the basic doctrine of the GKJTU.[3]

This *Twenty-First Century Update of the Heidelberg Catechism* has been written at the beginning of the 21st century. Therefore it is not impossible that one day this *Twenty-First Century Update of the Heidelberg Catechism* will be revised and further updated. Whereas the *Heidelberg Catechism* itself comprises the basic teaching for the reformational churches throughout all the ages.

This book has been written using simple language in a question-answer-format so that parishioners can get answers that are easy to understand. This book cannot explain every issue down to the last detail (in a casuistic way), but several concrete examples are mentioned to make it easier for parishioners to understand the issue.

These two books of doctrine of the GKJTU (The *Heidelberg Catechism* and its *Update*) should be used not only for catechism classes and confirmation classes, but also in other contexts, e.g. they are to be cited in sermons, read as a part of the liturgy, part by part printed in the parish news, discussed at Bible Studies and to be promoted through other church media.

We hope that this book will be helpful both for the members of the GKJTU and everyone who uses it. May it be a tool of the Lord as our church, the beloved GKJTU continues its journey.

Salatiga, in October 2008

---

[3] *Church Order of GKJTU,* Chapter II, article 3.2.

Twenty-First Century Update of the Heidelberg Catechism by the GKJTU

A. Realm of Culture

Question 1: What is the meaning of 'culture'?

Basically culture comprises the whole of human thought and activity, which is acquired by learning and habit, also all the outcome of these thoughts and activities.[4] That means that something becomes culture by a process of habitual acquisition, i.e. learning. As a simple example, the very act of eating cannot yet be regarded as culture, because eating is an instinctive, basic necessity. But if this eating becomes a festive ceremony with certain conventions, these conventions are an expression of culture.

This shows that culture is an expression of civilization which will be a common heritage.[a]

> a. **Genesis 4:20-22**: Adah bore Jabal; he was the ancestor of those who live in tents and have livestock. His brother's name was Jubal; he was the ancestor of all those who play the lyre and pipe. Zillah bore Tubal-cain, who made all kinds of bronze and iron tools. The sister of Tubal-cain was Naamah.

In detail culture comprises the following aspects:[5]

a) *The religious system and religious ceremonies*: Religion, faiths, myths and anything connected to spirituality.

b) *The social system*, comprising family systems, law systems, marriage, social organization etc.

c) *The system of knowledge,* both traditional and modern, as a means of human survival.

d) *Language* as a means of communication and expression of thought.

---

[4] *Translators' note:* The Indonesian understanding of culture is very much based on the etymology of the Indonesian word '*budaya*' ('culture') = '*budi daya*' ('reasoning and activity, effort'). Therefore the formula '(human) thought and activity' is again and again used in the following questions and answers.

[5] Koentjaraningrat, **Kebudayaan, Mentalitas, dan Pembangunan** [Indon.: *Culture, Mentality and Development*], Jakarta: PT Gramedia, 1984, page 2.

e) *Fine arts* as a means to express beauty, to make life meaningful and as a means of entertainment.
f) *The system of livelihood* to sustain personal and societal life.
g) *Technology and craftsmanship* to ameliorate human life.

Question 2: What is our attitude towards culture?

Individual Christians and the whole GKJTU have to develop two basic attitudes towards culture: *First of all,* all elements of culture should be received with a critical attitude. Culture is something concrete surrounding human life in its society. There is no society without culture, and no culture is static. Nevertheless, a critical and careful attitude is urgently needed. Christians and the Church have the task of discerning whether a specific aspect of culture is in accordance with the truth of the Word of God.[a] Through this process of testing, individual Christians and the church as a whole have to be capable of discerning what is 'light' and what is 'darkness', which one has to be abolished, which one can be received and which one needs to be renewed.[b]

> a. **Ephesians 5:10**: and try to discern what is pleasing to the Lord. (*English Standard Version*) – **1 Thessalonians 5:21**: but test everything; hold fast to what is good. – **1 John 4:1**: Beloved, do not believe every spirit, but test the spirits to see whether they are from God; for many false prophets have gone out into the world.
>
> b. **Genesis 1:4**: And God saw that the light was good; and God separated the light from the darkness.

The second step is to renew culture. Admittedly every element of culture contains some sin. The whole world, including its culture has fallen into sin.[c] It is the task of individual Christians and of the church as a whole to renew culture in the light of the Gospel, as a realization of the Christian new life, which is ready to be renewed again and again.

> c. **Romans 3:23**: all have sinned and are deprived of the glory of God. (*New American Bible*) – **1 John 5:19**: We know that we are God's children, and that the whole world lies under the power of the evil one. (Comp. *Heidelberg Catechism*, question no. 7).

Question 3: How can culture be renewed?

Basically every product of culture contains honorable values, but it is not impossible, that it also contains values contrary to the truths of the Christian faith. An example very familiar to the Javanese, especially in rural areas, is

A. Realm of Culture

the *kenduri*-ceremony.[6] For the Javanese this *kenduri*-ceremony is a means of salvation, both in this world and in the world to come. The *kenduri*-ceremony on the occasion of a death is a means of sending prayers for the dead so that the deceased might receive forgiveness and a place in heaven. During the *kenduri*-ceremony often prayers or invocations are offered to magical powers besides God, which are also called *danyang*.[a]

> a. **Leviticus 19:31**: Do not turn to ghosts and do not inquire of familiar spirits, to be defiled by them: I the LORD am your God. (*New Jewish Publishing Society Tanakh*) – **1 John 5:21**: Little children, keep yourselves from idols. – (Comp. *Heidelberg Catechism*, question no. 94-95).

The values of the *kenduri*-ceremonies as practiced in Javanese society are contradictory to the Christian faith. Nevertheless, the outer form of the *kenduri*-ceremonies, by which people are gathered, also contains positive values: Togetherness and harmony.

Thus to renew culture according to Christian faith basically means to use, to preserve and to develop both the outer form and the inner content of culture in accordance to Christian faith. That means that during the process of renewal, the outer form of culture may be preserved and developed, but its inner content may be abolished or changed so that it is befitting to Christian faith.[b]

---

[6] ***Translators' note:*** The so-called *kenduri-*, *kenduren-* or *selamatan*-ceremonies are cultic meals celebrated together with nearby (male) neighbors and relatives on the occasion of a birth, circumcision, marriage or death. During this ceremony, symbolic dishes are served, such as yellow rice, and prayers are offered to God (Allah), but often also to the traditional Javanese territorial spirits (tree spirits, house spirits etc.), the so-called *danyang*. In the prayers to God it is left open whether the God in Islamic, traditional Javanese, Hindu or Christian understanding is meant. The leftovers of the dishes are sometimes offered at graves and brought to neighbors not present at the ceremony (including Christian neighbors). Some Javanese Christians do not attend the *kenduri*-ceremonies and also do not eat the *kenduri*-dishes sent home to them. In recent years some fundamentalist Muslims also do not invite Christians to the *kenduri*-ceremonies nor would they send *kenduri*-dishes home to them. But most members of the GKJTU accept invitations to attend *kenduri*-ceremonies of their non-Christian neighbors in order not to offend them; but of course Christians would not follow non-Christian prayers. There are a few members and pastors of the GKJTU who also celebrate 'Christianized' *kenduri*-like feasts with a short Christian sermon and Christian prayers; even the *kenduri*-symbols are reinterpreted giving them a Christian meaning. The Catechism-Update tries to gently lead the members of the GKJTU to this third attitude.

b. **Romans 12:2**: Do not be conformed to this world, but be transformed by the renewing of your minds, so that you may discern what is the will of God – what is good and acceptable and perfect.

Question 4: What is the meaning of '*adat*'[7] and '*adat*-ceremonies'?[8]

The term '*adat*' comprises three fields of meaning:

First, regulations of customary law and the deeds resulting from that law, **secondly** customary manners and **thirdly** all forms of cultural ideas, which consist of cultural values, norms, laws and regulations which are interconnected and form a system. Whereas *adat*-ceremonies are all ceremonies connected with the *adat* of a certain society.

Question 5: What is our attitude towards '*adat*-ceremonies'?

There are two kinds of '*adat*-ceremonies': the basic ceremonies and the ceremonies connected with the cycle of life (rites of passage). The basic ceremonies are for the good of the whole society, such as the 'village cleansing' or '*nyadran*-ceremonies'.[9] The ceremonies connected with the cycle of life

---

[7] *Translators' note:* The Arabic-Indonesian loan word '*adat*' is commonly used by cultural anthropologists to mean a set of local and customary laws in Indonesian and Malay cultures, but also in some other Islamic and Hindu cultures in Asia; in a broader sense it is also used for customs and manners. Therefore this translation takes over the use of the term without translating it. The dictionary of the Indonesian language *Kamus Besar Bahasa Indonesia* (*Comprehensive Dictionary of the Indonesian Language*) mentions a threefold meaning of the word '*adat*', as explained above. In the Indonesian translation of the Bible the term '*adat*' is also used for Jewish and Israelite customs and manners (e.g. Judges 11:39; John 2:6), as obvious in the answer to question no. 8.

[8] *Translators' note:* Cultural anthropologists understand 'ceremonies', 'rituals' or 'rites' as symbolic actions prescribed by tradition, which contribute to the coherence of a group and provide identity and meaning for each member of that group. Mostly these symbolic actions also have a religious meaning. Ceremonies in connection with the cycle of life (birth, marriage, death etc.) are also called 'rites of passage'.

[9] *Translators' note:* During the 'village cleansing' or *nyadran* ceremony the whole village society gives thanks to the divine Creator and possibly to deities for the yield of the fields (or possibly fishing); at this occasion the village is also cleansed from the influence of all kinds of evil spirits. The '*mitoni*' or '*tingkeban*-ceremonies' are celebrated at the seventh month of pregnancy, the '*brokohan*-ceremonies' immediately after giving birth, the '*sepasaran*-ceremonies' 35 days after birth. By all these symbolic ceremonies people give thanks to God (Allah), and possibly also to deities and spirits, for the past protection and pray for further protection.

A. Realm of Culture

are more for the good of the individual, as e.g. the ceremonies connected to birth ('*mitoni*', '*tingkeban*', '*brokohan*', '*sepasaran*' etc.), ceremonies connected to marriage and ceremonies connected to burial.

These different '*adat*-ceremonies' are given realities which exist in a society as an outcome of human thought and activity. '*Adat*-ceremonies' than become a means for humans to relate to supernatural powers above in order to request protection, happiness and welfare. This is an indication that all humans have an inherent religious consciousness because they are created in the image of God and have been infused with the Spirit of God,[a] which is expressed by various '*adat*-ceremonies'.

> a. **Genesis 1:27**: So God created humankind in his image, in the image of God he created them; male and female he created them. – **Genesis 2:7**: then the LORD God formed man from the dust of the ground, and breathed into his nostrils the breath of life; and the man became a living being. (Comp. *Heidelberg Catechism*, question no. 6; *GKJTU-Update of the Heidelberg Catechism*, question no. 20 below).

Question 6: According to some people, '*adat*-ceremonies' are useful as a means of gaining wellbeing and getting saved.[10] Can man be saved by God through practicing '*adat* ceremonies'?

'Being saved' according to Christian faith means that humans return to a harmonious relationship with God as in the beginning of creation. According to this understanding it must be stressed that there is no kind of '*adat*-ceremonies' that can lead to eternal salvation.[a] Humans can attain salvation only by the grace of God, not through human efforts.[b]

> a. **Romans 3:20**: For no human being will be justified in his sight by works of the law, since through the law comes knowledge of sin. (*Revised Standard Version*). (Comp. *Heidelberg Catechism*, question no. 3, no. 5 and no. 13-14.
>
> b. **John 3:16-17**: For God so loved the world that he gave his only Son, so that everyone who believes in him may not perish but may have eternal life. Indeed, God did not send the Son into the world to condemn the world, but in order that the world might be saved through him. – **Romans 3:22-26**: the righteousness of God through faith in Jesus Christ for all who believe. For there is no distinction, since all have sinned and fall short of the glory of God; they are now justified by his grace as a gift, through the redemption that is in Christ Jesus, whom God

---

[10] *Translators' note:* The Arabic-Indonesian loan word '*selamat*' can either mean to be eternally saved or just to arrive safely somewhere – similar to the Hebrew term '*shalom*'. Especially in '*adat*-ceremonies' both meanings are present.

put forward as a sacrifice of atonement by his blood, effective through faith. He did this to show his righteousness, because in his divine forbearance he had passed over the sins previously committed; it was to prove at the present time that he himself is righteous and that he justifies the one who has faith in Jesus.

Question 7: *'Adat*-ceremonies' often are closely linked to sorcery, magic, forth telling, interpreting dreams etc. According to the Christian faith, do things like this determine human fate?

No, they cannot, because by fate we understand the future condition of somebody whether good or bad. This fate is not determined by spells, magic, divining, interpreting dreams etc. Believers are sure that their life is in the hand of God.[a] This does not mean that humans cannot determine their way of life. God has given humans responsibility for their life. Humans have the freedom to choose their way of life. This is the basis of Christian optimism: to believe in God's protection but nevertheless to be responsible to prepare for one's future. Christians must not abandon their hope in God and just rely on their own human efforts. At the same time, Christians must not abandon their human efforts and just surrender and depend on God.[b]

  a. **Matthew 6:25-34**: 'Therefore I tell you, do not worry about your life, what you will eat or what you will drink, or about your body, what you will wear. Is not life more than food, and the body more than clothing? Look at the birds of the air; they neither sow nor reap nor gather into barns, and yet your heavenly Father feeds them. Are you not of more value than they? And can any of you by worrying add a single hour to your span of life? And why do you worry about clothing? Consider the lilies of the field, how they grow; they neither toil nor spin, yet I tell you, even Solomon in all his glory was not clothed like one of these. But if God so clothes the grass of the field, which is alive today and tomorrow is thrown into the oven, will he not much more clothe you – you of little faith? Therefore do not worry, saying, "What will we eat?" or "What will we drink?" or "What will we wear?" For it is the Gentiles who strive for all these things; and indeed your heavenly Father knows that you need all these things. But strive first for the kingdom of God and his righteousness, and all these things will be given to you as well. So do not worry about tomorrow, for tomorrow will bring worries of its own. Today's trouble is enough for today.' – **Romans 14:7-9**: We do not live to ourselves, and we do not die to ourselves. If we live, we live to the Lord, and if we die, we die to the Lord; so then, whether we live or whether we die, we are the Lord's. For this end Christ died and lived again, so that he might be Lord of both the dead and the living. (Comp. *Heidelberg Catechism*, question no. 1 and no. 26-28).

  b. **Luke 14:31-33**: Or what king, going out to wage war against another king, will not sit down first and consider whether he is able with ten thousand to oppose the one who comes against him with twenty thousand? If he cannot, then, while the other is still far away, he sends a delegation and asks for the terms of peace. So therefore, none of you can become my disciple if you do not give up all your possessions.

Question 8: What is the attitude of individual Christians and of the church as a whole towards '*adat*-ceremonies' and everything connected with '*adat*', based on the understanding of the term explained above?

Christians are set free by Christ,[a] and therefore they are not to bind themselves to any kind of traditions or '*adat*-ceremonies'. On the basis of that freedom, Christians are given the liberty to discern, what is good and what is evil, what is beneficial and what is not, and to act accordingly.[b] Regarding '*adat*-ceremonies', individual Christians and the church as a whole should have the right attitude based on that Christian freedom.

- a. **Galatians 5:1**: For freedom Christ has set us free. Stand firm, therefore, and do not submit again to a yoke of slavery. – **Galatians 5:13**: You, my brothers, were called to be free. But do not use your freedom to indulge the sinful nature; rather, serve one another in love. (*New International Version*). (Comp. *Heidelberg Catechism*, question no. 34 and no. 91).
- b. **1 Corinthians 6:12**: 'All things are lawful for me,' but not all things are beneficial. 'All things are lawful for me,' but I will not be dominated by anything.

Firstly Christians can honor the '*adat*-ceremonies' as an outcome of human thought and activity in order to create interpersonal relations, relations with nature and with the powers above. Christians and the Church respect '*adat*-ceremonies' as beautiful, typical, complex and well-ordered outcomes of thought and activity. The Lord Jesus also respected '*adat*-ceremonies'; this was visible when e.g. he attended the marriage at Cana. As a good guest he attended the whole of the ceremony. Even when the ceremony got disturbed the Lord made a miracle to save the ceremony.[c]

- c. **John 2:1-11**

Secondly Christians receive '*adat*-ceremonies' with a critical attitude in the light of the Word of God. With this critical attitude individual Christians and the church as a whole can receive some '*adat*-ceremonies' completely, improve and change others, still others they will reject if those ceremonies are really in contrast to the Word of God.

Thirdly Christians renew and enlighten '*adat*-ceremonies'. Christians have become new creatures who are continually renewed,[d] and serve as lights of life.[e]

d. **Colossians 3:10:** and have clothed yourselves with the new self, which is being renewed in knowledge according to the image of its creator. (Comp. *Heidelberg Catechism*, question no. 45: "First, by His resurrection He has overcome death, ... Second, by His power we too are raised up to a new life. ..." Comp. also *Heidelberg Catechism*, question no. 86).

e. **Matthew 5:16:** In the same way, let your light shine before others, so that they may see your good works and give glory to your Father in heaven.

On this basis Christians have the task of renewing and enlightening '*adat*-ceremonies'. During that process Christians have to dare to change and reform all kinds of '*adat*-ceremonies' so that these ceremonies will be pleasing to God and useful to build up human life.[11]

Question 9: One '*adat*-ceremony' connected to the cycle of life is the wedding ceremony. What is the attitude of the Christian faith towards '*adat*-ceremonies' on the occasion of a wedding?

Wedding ceremonies can be found in the cultures of all nations as a part of '*adat*-ceremonies'. These wedding ceremonies are always connected with religion and religious beliefs. This shows that marriage has not only a universal human dimension, but also a sacral dimension. The Church acknowledges that a wedding is always adapted to local customs, therefore Christians should follow that '*adat*'. Nevertheless Christians should consider these ceremonies critically. Are they in conflict with the convictions of the Christian

---

[11] *Translators' note:* As mentioned in the annotation to question 3, some of the members and pastors of the GKJTU take quite different attitudes towards '*adat*-ceremonies': E.g. in some congregations of the GKJTU the 7th, 40th, 100th, and 1.000^{th} day after the death of a relative is commemorated with an '*adat*-ceremony', as these periods are similar to the phases of the mourning process as taught in modern pastoral counseling. As mentioned before these ceremonies are reinterpreted through Christian sermons and prayers, sometimes also the traditional symbols are still used but filled with a new meaning. Occult and magical practices are dropped. Christians and non-Christians attend these gatherings so that these ceremonies can become a means of evangelization. Similar things could be said concerning the ceremonies during pregnancy and after birth. Other Christians within the GKJTU reject these ceremonies first for pragmatic reasons, i.e. they regard these ceremonies simply as a waste of time and money, but secondly they also want to keep a distance from non-Christian '*adat*-ceremonies'.

A. Realm of Culture 29

faith? Thus, wedding ceremonies practiced by Christians need to be renewed according to the truth of the Christian faith.[12]

The Church acknowledges also that marriage has a sacral dimension, too. Notwithstanding the fact that GKJTU only acknowledges two sacraments, namely baptism and the Holy Supper,[13] nevertheless marriage has a clear spiritual i.e. divine dimension.[a] Marriage is according to the will and guidance of God. On this basis GKJTU blesses marriages by a special ceremony in church.

> a. **Matthew 19:6**: So they are no longer two, but one. Therefore what God has joined together, let not man divorce. *(Editor's translation based on the Indonesian official translation)* – **Ephesians 5:22-25**: Wives, be subject to your husbands as you are to the Lord. For the husband is the head of the wife just as Christ is the head of the church, the body of which he is the Savior. Just as the church is subject to Christ, so also wives ought to be, in everything, to their husbands. Husbands, love your wives, just as Christ loved the church and gave himself up for her.

Question 10: One expression of culture is the realm of marriage, which can vary widely depending on the local culture and various periods of history. What is our view concerning marriage?

Firstly, for believers marriage is willed by God. That means that the marriage of believers is holy because marriage was instituted by God.[a]

> a. **Genesis 2:18**: The LORD God said, "It is not good for the man to be alone. I will make a helper suitable for him." *(New International Version).*

---

[12] ***Translators' note:*** For example, during the Javanese wedding ceremony the bride and the bridegroom kneel before the parents of both and are blessed by them. This custom is practiced by many Javanese Christian couples, sometimes even in the church building. On the other hand according to the traditional Javanese wedding ceremony the bride symbolically feeds the husband in order to show her servility to him; some Javanese Christian couples in contrast feed each other to symbolize that they will serve each other. Whereas the dousing of the bride with "holy water" is rejected as too magical by many Javanese Christians, other Javanese Christians might regard it as just a symbol of purity. Also in this respect the attitudes of Javanese Christians and pastors differ widely, so that often not only spiritual but also practical considerations are taken into account. The Catechism-Update deliberately does not want to ban or to suggest certain ceremonies. The main point is that the ceremonies chosen and practiced ceremonies are reinterpreted – and if necessary modified – in the light of the Gospel.

[13] Comp. **Heidelberg Catechism,** question no. 68.

Therefore the believers have to safeguard the institution of marriage in order that its sanctity is kept.^b

> b. **1 Corinthians 7:2**: But because of the temptation to sexual immorality, each man should have his own wife and each woman her own husband. (*English Standard Version*). (Comp. *Heidelberg Catechism,* question no. 108-109).

Secondly marriage should be in the form of monogamy, one husband with one wife, until death. So Christian faith does not acknowledge divorce except by death.[14] The marriage covenant is for life. Therefore temporary marriage, 'contract marriage'[15] etc. cannot be justified.

---

[14] *Translators' note:* In Indonesian the distinction between divorce and widowhood is very subtle. The Indonesian word used for 'widow' ('*janda*') can denote either a divorced woman ('*janda cerai hidup*' – 'divorced alive') or a widow in the usual sense, whose husband has deceased ('*janda cerai mati*' – 'divorced by death'); the same can be said for the word 'widower' ('*duda*'). This language phenomenon reflects the loose Islamic law on divorce. In this context the liturgical formula "until death do you part / divorce" has a special significance, and is therefore also used in answer no. 10. The verse from Matthew 19:6 can be found on almost every wedding card of Indonesian Christians, in the specific wording of Indonesian (and German or Dutch) translations: "what God has joined together, let not man divorce", which has also been cited in connection with question no. 9 above.

Of course cases happen in the pastoral care of GKJTU where divorce seems almost inevitable, if e.g. one spouse is permanently abused or has been deserted or one spouse is notoriously unfaithful (cp. Mt 5:32; 19:9). In the *Bylaws to the Church Order of the GKJTU,* § XIII, Article 42, sentence 7-8, the remarriage of divorced spouses is explicitly regulated. But after some discussions the GKJTU has decided not to mention such exceptions in the Catechism-Update in order not to open a back door too quick and too wide.

[15] *Translators' note:* Especially some expatriates working in Indonesia on a contract basis also sign a temporary 'wedding contract' with an Indonesian woman, according to the time limit of their working contract. Such a marriage is automatically dissolved upon completion of its term as mentioned in the wedding contract and no divorce is necessary. Such 'temporary contract marriages' (Arab.: *nikah mut'ah*) are allowed according to Islamic Shi'a-Law on the basis of Surah 4:24, but according to Islamic Sunni-Law 'temporary marriages' are identical with prostitution. The majority of Islamic and public lawyers in Indonesia reject such temporary 'contract marriages'. According to the actual Indonesian Law, such 'marriage contracts' have no legal force; a new legal draft is being prepared which even sets penalties for such 'contract marriages' and anyone involved in them. 'Contract marriages' are unanimously rejected by Indonesian churches, nevertheless some church members may practice such 'contract marriages'. But such 'contract marriages' are mostly practiced in big cities such as Jakarta, Surabaya etc., where the GKJTU has no congregations yet. Therefore this problem is not yet very relevant for the GKJTU.

A. Realm of Culture

Question 11: Another ceremony connected with the cycle of life is circumcision.[16] What is our view of circumcision?

According to the Bible, circumcision was first of all the sign of God's covenant with Abraham,[a] long before the Mosaic Law was given to the Israelites.[b]

    a. **Genesis 17:10**: This is my covenant, which you shall keep, between me and you and your offspring after you: Every male among you shall be circumcised.

    b. **Galatians 3:16-18**: Now the promises were made to Abraham and to his offspring; ... the law, which came four hundred thirty years later, does not annul a covenant previously ratified by God, so as to nullify the promise. For if the inheritance comes from the law, it no longer comes from the promise; but God granted it to Abraham through the promise.

---

[16] *Translators' note:* Long before the arrival of Islam in the archipelago which is nowadays called Indonesia, the Javanese (and many other ethnic groups) practiced circumcision as a 'Rite of Passage', a ceremony to mark the transition from boyhood to manhood, which was also celebrated with a ceremonial meal. Therefore the Javanese language also has its own word for circumcision (*'tetak'* / *'supit'*), whereas the Indonesian language has borrowed the Arabic words *'sunat'* and *'khitanan'* for circumcision. Until today Hindu and Buddhist Javanese practice circumcision, too. Educated Muslims know about that. Nevertheless the broad majority of Indonesians regard circumcision as an Islamic rite, 'to circumcise' is often regarded identical with 'to convert someone to Islam'. Because of this background and because of a very literal understanding of Gal. 5:1-12 Javanese (and other) churches forbade circumcision until recently.

Nowadays many different positions can be found among the congregations and leaders of the GKJTU and other Indonesian churches: In a few Christian congregations circumcision is celebrated with a great feast, most Javanese Christians circumcise their children discreetly in hospital 'for reasons of health', but in a few other congregations circumcision is still a reason for church discipline.

In such a situation the *GKJTU-Update of the Heidelberg Catechism* can give some suggestions only: From the wordings of the question it is already made clear that circumcision should be understood as a 'ceremony connected with the cycle of life' (rite of passage), not as a specific Islamic or Jewish rite. Then the biblical positions in this question are briefly made clear. According to reformed tradition and on the basis of Col. 2:11-12 circumcision is connected with baptism. Without giving a direct command, the *Catechism-Update* tries to open the way for a further consensus among the congregations.

But later on Judaism connected circumcision with the Mosaic Law and understood it as a way of salvation. It was this Judaist understanding which Paul rejected in his epistle to the Galatians.[c]

- c. **Galatians 5:2b-3**: If you let yourselves be circumcised, Christ will be of no benefit to you. Once again I testify to every man who lets himself be circumcised that he is obliged to obey the entire law.

What's more, the sign of the new covenant is baptism, not circumcision.[d]

- d. **Colossians 2:11-12a**: In him you were also circumcised, in the putting off of the sinful nature, not with a circumcision done by the hands of men but with the circumcision done by Christ, having been buried with him in baptism ... (*New International Version*). (Comp. ***Heidelberg Catechism***, question no. 74)

In many other passages in his letters Paul makes statements concerning the controversy about circumcision, e.g. in 1 Corinthians,[e] or when he had Timothy circumcised in order to facilitate the propagation of the Gospel.[f]

- e. **1 Corinthians 7:19**: To be circumcised is of no importance, and to be uncircumcised is of no importance; what is important is the keeping of God's commandments. (*New Jerusalem Bible*, comp. Col. 3:11)

- f. **Acts 16:1-3**: Paul went on also to Derbe and to Lystra, where there was a disciple named Timothy, ... Paul wanted Timothy to accompany him; and he took him and had him circumcised because of the Jews who were in those places, for they all knew that his father was a Greek.

Question 12: In order to promote harmony in society all citizens, including Christians, will be involved in all kinds of social activities, such as communal work, mutual helping among neighbors, funerals, help in natural disasters, activities as a board member of a social organization etc. Are Christians allowed to be diverted by these activities from attending a church service?[17]

---

[17] *Translators' note:* Mutual help, assistance for neighbors (Indon. '*sambatan*') and common work for civil projects (Indon. '*gotong royong*') are one of the basic values of the Indonesian state philosophy, the '*Pancasila*'. That common work for civil projects very often is requested on Sunday mornings, when the air is still fresh, many people (at least the civil servants and some employees) have a day off and the Muslim majority has had their Friday Prayers. Because of these reasons weddings, meetings of civil organizations and sport activities are very often held on Sunday morning, too. In the bigger city congregations the Christians can assist a civil project on Sunday morning and then go to church in the afternoon; but in the smaller village congregations there is usually just one Sunday service at 7 o'clock in the morning,

A. Realm of Culture

Attending church service is one expression of love and reverence to God.[a] But God also wishes men to express their love to Him through loving their neighbors.[b]

> a. **Exodus 23:25:** You shall worship the LORD your God, ... – **Hebrews 10:25:** ... We should not stay away from our assembly, as is the custom of some, but encourage one another, and this all the more as you see the day drawing near. (*New American Bible*). (Comp. *Heidelberg Catechism*, question no. 103).
>
> b. **Mark 12:30-31:** '... you shall love the Lord your God with all your heart, and with all your soul, and with all your mind, and with all your strength.' The second is this, 'You shall love your neighbor as yourself.' There is no other commandment greater than these. (Comp. *Heidelberg Catechism*, question no. 111).

One form of expression love for their neighbor is through active involvement in social activities.[c]

> c. **Matthew 25:40:** The King will reply, 'I tell you the truth, whatever you did for one of the least of these brothers of mine, you did for me.' (*New International Version*).

That means, God wishes a balanced and holistic service of the believers, both ritual service at church as well as social service. So, could this social service become more important than ritual service at church? That question cannot be simply answered by 'yes' or 'no', but it requires a careful consideration of all aspects of love. If that social activity is planned and scheduled in advance, of course these activities should not become an impediment for church attendance, as the social activities can be scheduled before or after the church service. But if these social activities are very urgent and sudden and happen to be simultaneous to church service then the presbytery as the body responsible for devotional life has to take adequate and special measures.

Question 13: Other expressions of culture are the traditional fine arts, such as '*reog*', '*wayang*', '*ludruk*', '*ketoprak*', '*campursari*' et al. What is the attitude of GKJTU members towards these expressions of fine arts?

Fine arts are a part of culture and one of the characteristics of human life. Only humans can create fine arts and express beauty through several kinds

---

so that Christians get in trouble with their conscience. The GKJTU Update hands this question over to the respective presbytery (congregation church council).

of fine arts.[18] So it is one of the signs that man was created in the image of God. Thus fine arts originate from God because they are born out of the extraordinary dignity of humans as being made in the image of God.

Starting from this basic understanding, believers have the following attitude towards fine arts, both traditional and modern:

First they respect every work of art as an outcome of human thought and activity. Fine arts are a visual and auditory expression of human feelings and thoughts which are presented as forms of beauty. Yet these forms of beauty

---

[18] *Translators' note:* '*Reog*' is a dance-drama from Ponorogo (East Java), during which the main dancer uses a heavy frightening lion mask weighing about 50kg, accompanied by several other male and female dancers. During the dance-drama the sprits are enchanted, in order that the dancers fall into a trance and can eat shards, unopened coconuts etc. '*Wayang*' is a form of traditional Javanese drama, mostly in ancient Javanese language, depicting stories based on Hindu epic literature and Javanese mythology; it is performed either by human actors ('*wayang orang*'), mostly by leather puppets ('*wayang kulit*'), sometimes by wooden puppets ('*wayang golek*') or other media. '*Ketoprak*' is a second kind of drama from Central Java, depicting stories mainly from Javanese history, using a more modern form of the Javanese language. '*Ludruk*' is another kind of drama, originating from East Java, but in contrast to '*ketoprak*' it is dealing with contemporary subjects, using even more contemporary, plain Javanese language and more modern dress. All these forms of Javanese drama are accompanied by Javanese singers and the '*gamelan*-orchestra', consisting of different kinds of gongs, xylophones, stringed instruments, drums etc. The more traditional these performing arts are, the more traditional mantras and offerings for the spirits are used. '*Campursari*' is a mixture of traditional Javanese and modern musical elements and instruments (gamelan, keyboard, violin, guitar etc.) which has become popular in Java since the last decade of the 20th century. In the past Javanese Christians were forbidden to perform or attend most of these traditional Javanese fine arts because of the spiritual background of these arts.

Unfortunately in the present wording of the answer to question 13 the problem of this spiritual background is not discussed very much. In the concrete life of the GKJTU there are several practitioners of traditional arts, who of course will not use mantras and offerings to the spirits. At common performances e.g. at village festivities the non-Christian artists might perform these magical practices, but Christian artists stay away as far as possible from such practices. At special festival services of the GKJTU sometimes gamelan orchestras, '*Wayang*-shadowplay' groups, dance groups etc. contribute to the program, and these groups sometimes consist of Christians and non-Christians. On these occasions the non-Christian artists also refrain from mantras, offerings etc., but they have the opportunity to hear the Word of God and many have come to faith thereby. On the one hand fundamentalist Islam during the last decades has condemned the traditional arts more and more, whereas the Javanese churches since the middle of the 20th century have come to appreciate the traditional arts more and more. This has caused more and more artists to be attracted to Christianity.

are also influenced by the surrounding context. The Javanese e.g. can fully comprehend and enjoy '*gamelan*-music', whereas Europeans may not be able to enjoy it. Nevertheless, a believer respects and honors certain works of art and does not see them negatively, even though he/she cannot (yet) fully comprehend it because of its alien background.

Secondly believers should be able to evaluate works of art. A work of art should be evaluated from two aspects, i.e. beauty and meaning. A quality artwork is both beautiful and meaningful. The Christians should not only regard the beauty and delight a specific artwork gives but also look at its meaning. A song e.g. might have a beautiful and pleasant melody but it can be worthless because of its foul lyrics.

Thirdly, believers should become practitioners of the fine arts. Not everyone is gifted for the fine arts. Therefore all gifts in the field of arts have to be nourished and developed as an expression of gratitude towards God.[a] On this basis with every expression of art the ideal of meaningful beauty has to be kept in mind, in the sense of beauty that builds up human life so that it becomes full of dignity.

   a. **Matthew 25:23**: His master said to him, 'Well done, good and faithful servant; you have been faithful over a little, I will set you over much; enter into the joy of your master!' (*Revised Standard Version*).

Question 14: In the field of musical arts sometimes new lyrics are combined with an already known melody (which is called *kontrafaktur* by the experts).[19] What is our attitude towards this?

---

[19] ***Translators' note:*** Traditionally a '*contrafactura*' is a spiritual song written to a secular melody (or vice versa), as in the past some well-known spiritual hymns were written to melodies of secular folk songs, but also vice versa, as e.g. the melody of the well-known hymn "What a Friend We Have in Jesus" has been used for the Indonesian nationalist song '*Ibu Pertiwi*', which deplores the fate of Indonesia under colonial rule. Sometimes newer church hymns also use the melodies of older church hymns and psalms. The Indonesian term '*kontrafaktur*' or the Dutch '*contrafact*' can be used to describe any song written to a melody from another composer. Whereas the English term '*contrafact(ion)*' describes a new musical composition built out of an already existing one, most often a new melody overlaid on a familiar harmonic structure, as done in modern Jazz music. For Javanese Christians this question became virulent when the melody of the quite indecent Javanese song '*Manuk Cucak Rawa*' was used for a Christian popular song. '*Manuk Cucak Rawa*' literally speaks about some kind of song-bird (*Pycnonotus zeylanicus* – Straw-headed Bulbul), but it might also refer to the male genitals. The answer to question

Basically any artwork deserves respect. One of the most important forms of respect is not to steal this intellectual property and not to copy it illegally, because every artwork is the intellectual property of its creator.[a]

> a. **1 Corinthians 6:10**: nor thieves nor the greedy ... nor swindlers will inherit the kingdom of God. (Comp. *Heidelberg Catechism*, question no. 110).

In the field of music it is even a theft of intellectual property to use the melody of an already known song for a new song, because that melody is the intellectual property of someone, therefore it cannot be used at the discretion of somebody else – even if it might be used for honorable purposes, as for a church service, educational purposes, social aid etc. Such usage can only be permitted with the consent of the composer or his family. Therefore it is best to create new songs, with a new melody and new lyrics, to glorify the name of the Lord.[b]

> b. **Psalm 149:1**: Praise the LORD! Sing to the LORD a new song, his praise in the assembly of the faithful.

Question 15: Clothing is also a form of art. What is our view concerning clothing?

Clothing has many aspects. It serves not only to cover the body and protect it. Clothing also has an aesthetic aspect, an aspect of decency and even of morals. Therefore believers will take care that they are decently dressed out of self-respect and honor to God, the creator of human bodies, also as a kind of expression of respect towards others.[a]

> a. **Romans 13:13-14**: Let us behave decently, as in the daytime, not in orgies and drunkenness, not in sexual immorality and debauchery, not in dissension and jealousy. Rather, clothe yourselves with the Lord Jesus Christ, and do not think about how to gratify the desires of the sinful nature. (*New International Version*). – **1 Thessalonians 4:12a:** ... that you may behave properly toward outsiders ...

A Javanese proverb says "*Ajining raga saka busana*" ("External esteem originates in the clothing"),[20] which means that the self-esteem towards

---

14 concentrates very much on the legal aspect of the problem, but gives also an outlook onto spiritual and intellectual creativity.

[20] ***Translators' note***: At least from the 19th century on until today Javanese culture (and the cultures of some other ethnic groups in Indonesia) has been very much concerned with appropriate dress, influenced by Islam but also by the 'Victorian' morals of the former colonial society in the Netherlands' Indies (which also means an indirect influence of Calvinist-pietistic morals). The quoted proverb means that appropriate (not necessarily luxurious) clothing is an expression of self-esteem but

A. Realm of Culture

one's own body is determined by proper clothing, appropriate to the occasion and local culture.[b] Believers should also take care that they do not become a stumbling block to others and tempt them to sin.[c]

- b. **Isaiah 52:1a:** Awake, awake, put on your strength, O Zion! Put on your beautiful garments, O Jerusalem, the holy city; … – **1 Timothy 2:9a:** … also that the women should dress themselves modestly and decently in suitable clothing, …

- c. **1 Corinthians 8:9:** But take care that this liberty of yours does not somehow become a stumbling block to the weak.

Question 16: So far we have discussed many issues of Javanese culture. Is the GKJTU indeed a church for the Javanese only?

No, it is not. Although the Christian Church from North Central Java (Gereja Kristen Jawa Tengah Utara – GKJTU) came into being in the Javanese region and the majority of its members are Javanese, nevertheless from its very beginning until today the GKJTU also has included Chinese, Batak, Ambonese, Sangirese, Toraja, Balinese and several other ethnic groups.[21] The

---

leads also to esteem by others. The Chinese minority in Java and other ethnic groups in Indonesia have different dress codes. Therefore some Christian women (and men) predominantly from the above mentioned ethnic groups become a stumbling block because of their inappropriate, scanty clothing (which is seen as inappropriate by the Javanese and other ethnic and religious groups). But sometimes Javanese Christians are also influenced by the clothing manners of the above mentioned ethnic groups or by foreigners. On the other hand fundamentalist Muslims demand the total veiling of women. The wearing of the headscarf is already compulsory for civil servants, school girls etc. in the provinces of Aceh, West-Sumatra and other regions of Indonesia. Also the first drafts for the new Pornography Law had such a tendency, but this cannot be found in the wording of the law passed in October 2008.

21 *Translators' note:* The Javanese people live predominantly in the central and eastern part of the Island of Java, which is therefore called '*Tanah Jawa*' – 'The land of the Javanese'. They use their regional language Javanese and the national language Indonesian, which are languages as closely related as English is to German. Within the GKJTU both languages are used, but many Javanese (especially from the younger generation) have difficulty understanding the high Javanese language used in the church or at official occasions. In addition as a result of the impact of globalization, the Indonesian language (and even more so) the Javanese language and culture has become more and more influenced or even replaced by a kind of 'world culture' under US-American dominance.

As decided by the 26th General Synod Assembly of the GKJTU, the name GKJTU should be translated as "Christian Church from North Central Java" to make clear that the GKJTU historically originated in North Central Java, but it is not a church exclusively for the Javanese or restricted to the area of North Central Java. Although

Christian Church from North Central Java actually has its domicile in the Northern part of Central Java, but it is not a Javanese ethnic church. Therefore GKJTU appreciates the variety of languages and cultures as a gift from God.[a]

> a. **Psalm 86:9**: All the nations you have made shall come and bow down before you, O Lord, and shall glorify your name. – **Acts of the Apostles 17:26**: And he made from one every nation of men to live on all the face of the earth, having determined allotted periods and the boundaries of their habitation. (*Revised Standard Version*).

These local languages, cultures and their fine arts should be cultivated as a means of worship.[b]

> b. **Psalm 117:1**: Praise the LORD, all you nations! Extol him, all you peoples! (Comp. further Psalm 57:10; 66:8; 67:1-8; 102:23; 108:3; Romans 15:9-12).

For the sake of evangelism, members of GKJTU study and cultivate the language and the culture of every ethnic group to be reached with the gospel.[c] Thus the cultures and languages within the GKJTU have become more and more diverse.

> c. **Psalm 96:3**: Declare his glory among the nations, his marvelous works among all the peoples. – **1 Corinthians 9:20-23**: To the Jews I became as a Jew, in order to win Jews. … I have become all things to all people, that I might by all means save some. I do it all for the sake of the gospel, so that I may share in its blessings. (Comp. further Psalm 9:11; 105:1; Isaiah; 51:4; Matthew 28:18-20).

Question 17: Why does the GKJTU esteem high the diversity of culture and language?

God created the world and all that is in it in plurality. Thus diversity is a basic feature of creation which has to be accepted with praise and respected. All efforts of humans to make that plurality uniform neglect the very essence of life.

In the Old Testament humans once tried to unite and make mankind uniform by building a tower which was meant as a central point of orientation for human life. But God was not pleased with that plan, therefore he confused

---

at least 95% of the members of the GKJTU are Javanese, other Indonesian ethnic groups can be found also within the GKJTU. According to question and answer 16-17 this variety of ethnic groups with their languages and cultures should be cultivated in the GKJTU although GKJTU is still far from its ideal goal of giving these other languages and cultures an equal footing with the Javanese.

A. Realm of Culture

their language. As a result, they became scattered to the ends of the earth and developed their distinctive characteristics.[a]

   a. **Genesis 11:1-9**.

Since then the Lord has spoken to humans according to their respective cultures and languages.[b]

   b. **Acts of the Apostles 2:8-11**: … we hear, each of us, in our own native language … Parthians, Medes, Elamites, and residents of Mesopotamia, Judea and Cappadocia, Pontus and Asia, Phrygia and Pamphylia, Egypt and the parts of Libya belonging to Cyrene, and visitors from Rome, both Jews and proselytes, Cretans and Arabs – in our own languages we hear them speaking about God's deeds of power.

Although in Christ all nations and ethnic groups have become united,[c] that does not mean that their distinctive cultures and languages have become uniform. On the contrary, until the End different ethnic groups will always praise the Lord in their diverse cultures and languages.[d]

   c. **Colossians 3:11**: In that renewal there is no longer Greek and Jew, circumcised and uncircumcised, barbarian, Scythian, slave and free; but Christ is all and in all!

   d. **Revelation 7:9-10**: After this I looked, and there was a great multitude that no one could count, from every nation, from all tribes and peoples and languages, standing before the throne and before the Lamb, robed in white, with palm branches in their hands. They cried out in a loud voice, saying, "Salvation belongs to our God who is seated on the throne, and to the Lamb!"

As a result of globalization, the cultures of the nations and ethnic groups are becoming more and more uniform, both on a national and an international level. But the GKJTU does not want to be carried away by this torrent of cultural uniformity. On the contrary GKJTU will always appreciate and cultivate local cultures.

B. Realm of Religious Plurality and the Diversity of Christian Churches

Question 18: What is meant by 'plurality' and 'pluralism'?

'Plurality' just denotes the variety found in reality. In Indonesia a huge variety of ethnic groups, skin colors, religions, languages etc. can be found,[22] whereas 'pluralism' is a view or attitude concerning this variety found in reality. The GKJTU accepts pluralism as a means to accept and appreciate diversity.[a]

a. **1 Corinthians 12:1-31**.

The plurality found in Indonesia, especially the different religions, desperately needs pluralism to facilitate living together in mutual respect.[23] This

---

[22] *Translators' note:* Ethnic and religious diversity is one of the greatest challenges for church, state and society in Indonesia. '*Bhinneka Tunggal Ika*' ('Unity in Diversity') is therefore written as a motto on the national coat of arms of Indonesia. The modern Indonesian language has developed a highly variegated vocabulary to describe this diversity, a vocabulary which cannot always be given an exact English equivalent in this translation.

[23] *Translators' note:* In most languages 'pluralism' is a term with various meanings. According to *Merriam-Webster's Collegiate Online Dictionary,* 2009, it can mean either: "**1:** the holding of two or more offices ... at the same time **2:** the quality or state of being plural **3** ... a theory that there are more than one or more than two kinds of ultimate reality ... **4a:** a state of society in which members of diverse ethnic, racial, religious, or social groups maintain ... participation in and development of their traditional culture ... **b:** a concept, doctrine, or policy advocating this state". In the third meaning according to *Merriam-Webster's*, pluralism can even neglect the existence of any binding, objective and ultimate truth.

In Indonesia the debate on pluralism has become much polarized by a '*fatwa*' ('decision on Islamic Law') issued in 2005 by the Indonesian Council of Scholars of Islamic Law ('*Majelis Ulama Indonesia*' – MUI). This '*fatwa*' rejects pluralism as "a view sustaining that all religions are the same and therefore all religious truths are relative ... also that the adherents of all religions go to heaven ..." On the one hand there are indeed some Islamic and Christian theologians in Indonesia who hold the view that all religions hold truths of the same value and are equivalent ways to eternal salvation. On the other hand the above mentioned '*fatwa*' of MUI is one reason why fundamentalist Islamic groups are agitating for more and more brutal treatment of other Islamic groups or other religious communities –primarily against Christians.

The GKJTU in its Catechism-Update rejects such fundamentalism in the sense of the MUI *fatwa,* but does not embrace a liberal pluralistic theology of religions. The plurality is a challenge permitted by God so that the faith of the believers might be constantly put to the test.[b]

  b. **Judges 2:21-22**: I will no longer drive out before them any of the nations ... In order to test Israel, whether or not they would take care to walk in the way of the LORD as their ancestors did.

Question 19: The different religions are one form of plurality within Indonesian society. What is actually meant by the term 'religion'?

Religion is a system which regulates faith, the adoration of the Almighty God, also the rules of interaction with fellow men and the environment.[24] In every religion there are four basic components, i.e. dogmas, rituals, ethics and a religious community. Dogmas are the basic teachings concerning God and salvation. Rituals are the forms of worship towards God. Ethics are the teachings concerning an ideal lifestyle according to the will of God as understood by that specific religion. A religious community is a group of adherents of a specific religion.

Question 20: What is our view concerning religion?

Religion is one of the distinctives of man, which man uses to foster his relationship with God. This is called religious conscience and can be explained as follows: Man was created as "the LORD God ... breathed into his nostrils the breath of life",[a] so that in every human being there is a divine element, which since than always calls man to come back and enter into a relationship with God.[b]

  a. **Genesis 2:7**: Then the LORD God formed man from the dust of the ground, and breathed into his nostrils the breath of life; and the man became a living being.

  b. **Ecclesiastes 3:11:** Also He has put eternity in their hearts, ... (*New King James Version*).

Man was created in the image of God, that means that some of the attributes of God were put into man.[c] Being created in the image of God, man will always search for God as his 'true, genuine image'. During this search man

---

GKJTU has put limits to its definition of 'pluralism' as being 'to accept and appreciate diversity', which would be meaning no. 4b according to *Merriam-Webster's*.

[24] See article '*agama*' ('religion') in *Kamus Besar Bahasa Indonesia (Comprehensive Dictionary of the Indonesian Language)*, 3rd edition.

B. Realm of Religious Plurality and the Diversity of Christian Churches 43

creates religion as a means to know God.[25] Nevertheless, religion is not only about man believing in God, but also about the task of man to shape his life in this world according to his will.[d]

> c. **Genesis 1:27:** So God created humankind in his image, in the image of God he created them; male and female he created them. (Comp. *Heidelberg Catechism*, question no. 6; *GKJTU-Update to the Heidelberg Catechism*, question no. 5).
>
> d. **Matthew 22:37-39:** He said to him, 'You shall love the Lord your God with all your heart, and with all your soul, and with all your mind.' This is the greatest and first commandment. And a second is like it: 'You shall love your neighbor as yourself.' ...

Question 21: According to the Christian faith, where does religious plurality come from?

After the fall, mankind has tried in various ways to come back to God. In their attempts to restore their relationship with God, men create various methods, which are then called religions, according to their respective context.[a]

> a. **Genesis 4:3-7:** In the course of time Cain brought to the LORD an offering of the fruit of the ground, and Abel for his part brought of the firstlings of his flock, their fat portions. And the LORD had regard for Abel and his offering, but for Cain and his offering he had no regard. So Cain was very angry, and his countenance fell. The LORD said to Cain, "Why are you angry, and why has your countenance fallen? If you do well, will you not be accepted? And if you do not do well, sin is lurking at the door; its desire is for you, but you must master it."– **Acts of the Apostles 17:22-23:** Then Paul stood in front of the Areopagus and said, "Athenians, I see how extremely religious you are in every way. For as I went through the city and looked carefully at the objects of your worship, I found among them an altar with the inscription, 'To an unknown god.' What therefore you worship as unknown, this I proclaim to you." – **Romans 2:14-16:** When Gentiles, who do not possess the law, do instinctively what the law requires, these, though not having the law, are a law to themselves. They show that what the law requires is written on their hearts, to which their own conscience also bears witness; and their conflicting thoughts will accuse or perhaps excuse them on the day when, according to my gospel, God, through Jesus Christ, will judge the secret thoughts of all.

God also has revealed himself to mankind in various ways.[b]

---

[25] *Translators' note:* The answer to question no. 20 deliberately regards religion from man's point of view as 'created by man'. But then the answer to question no. 21 mentions also about divine revelation, until finally the answer to question no. 22 leads to the sentence: "no religion whatsoever can save a human. Humans can only be saved by the initiative of God ... by the life and death of / with Jesus Christ."

b. **Romans 1:19-20:** For what can be known about God is plain to them, because God has shown it to them. Ever since the creation of the world his eternal power and divine nature, invisible though they are, have been understood and seen through the things he has made. So they are without excuse. – **Acts of the Apostles 14:16-17:** In past generations he allowed all the nations to follow their own ways; yet he has not left himself without a witness in doing good – giving you rains from heaven and fruitful seasons, and filling you with food and your hearts with joy.

On the other hand the devil tries in various ways to draw men away from God.^{c} Temporarily God has been tolerating this variety,^{d} until in the end he has revealed His Word in Jesus Christ, in order "that at the name of Jesus every knee should bend, in heaven and on earth and under the earth".^{e}

c. **1 Corinthians 10:20:** what they sacrifice, they sacrifice to demons ... (*New American Bible*).

d. **Deuteronomy 4:19b:** ... the sun, the moon, and the stars. The LORD your God has given these to all other peoples for them to worship. (*Today's English Version*).

e. **Philippians 2:10 – Hebrews 1:1-2:** In many and various ways God spoke of old to our fathers by the prophets; but in these last days he has spoken to us by a Son, whom he appointed the heir of all things, through whom also he created the world. (comp. *Five Documents of Unity – Declaration of Common Understanding of Christian Faith in Indonesia,* paragraph. 6 and 16 in the 1990 and 1994 versions = paragraph II.2.3.1.2 und II.2.3.5.2 in the *Document of Unity 2000*).[26]

---

[26] *Translators' note:* As mentioned in the Translators' Preface, the Communion of Churches in Indonesia (*Persekutuan Gereja-gereja Indonesia* – PGI), of which GKJTU is a member, received a common creed in 1984, the "Declaration of Common Understanding of Christian Faith in Indonesia". This declaration until today is one of the *(Five) Documents of Unity* of the PGI-churches. At its revision in 1990 all of part V: "The Kingdom of God and New Life" was added. Within this part it is stated in paragraph 16: "The Kingdom of God will only be completely revealed when 'at the name of Jesus every knee should bow, in heaven and on earth and under the earth, and every tongue should confess that Jesus Christ is Lord, to the glory of God the Father' (Phil. 2:10-11). Also in the part on creation the Scripture reference of Phil. 2:10 was added in paragraph 6. At the revisions in 1994 and 2000 these parts were left unaltered – although some pluralistic Indonesian theologians might have some objections against it. But before and during the 13th General Assembly of PGI in 2000 the *Five Documents of Unity* were thoroughly revised, renamed as *Document of Unity* and their structure changed. Therefore the above mentioned passages now are to be found in paragraph II.2.3.1.2 and II.2.3.5.2 of the actual version of the "Declaration of Common Understanding of Christian Faith in Indonesia". Unfortunately in the collection *Reformed Witness Today,* ed. Lukas Vischer, an English

B. Realm of Religious Plurality and the Diversity of Christian Churches 45

Question 22: What is our attitude towards the plurality of religions?

First, the variety of religions is a concrete reality and a universal phenomenon. Christians cannot close their eyes to this reality. It is this very reality that the church is forced to always understand, be aware of and struggle with, so that the church can take the right attitude in the midst of that variety.

Secondly the church respects, but does not regard all religions as one and the same. Every religion is unique. Nevertheless every religion basically teaches a way of salvation by its doctrine, rituals and ethics. Although the Christian faith holds the view that no religion whatsoever can save a human.[27] Humans can only be saved by the initiative of God, not by human

---

translation only of the 1984 version can be found, where the Scripture references of Phil. 2:10-11 were not yet included.

By explicitly citing Phil. 2:10 in its answer to this question 21, the GKJTU is not only based on Scriptural authority, but is also in communion with its sister churches in Indonesia.

[27] ***Translators' note:*** As mentioned in the translators' note to question no. 18, one of the most important challenges of the church and theology in Indonesia is the issue of the uniqueness of Christian faith in the midst of religious pluralism. Among Indonesian Christian theologians very different answers are given to this question. The GKJTU tries to give a cautious, balanced answer with no arrogance, based on Biblical evidence. A careful distinction is made between common sense statements and specific statements of Christian faith. Regarding the question about the uniqueness of Christian faith the GKJTU gives a very plain answer: "Every religion is unique" – which is common sense among Christian and Non-Christian theologians in Indonesia. Still common sense is the statement: "Humans can only be saved by the initiative of God". But this sentence is followed by the Christian creed "that salvation can only be obtained by the life and death of Jesus Christ", based on Acts 4:12. This sentence is traditionally understood that humans can only be saved because of the vicarious suffering and death of Christ. But the wording of the GKJTU can also be understood and translated to mean that humans are saved by living with Christ until their death. Thus it is made clear that saving faith is not just lip service to a certain creed or formal membership in a Christian church, but "henceforth, to live unto" Christ (comp. *Heidelberg Catechism*, question no. 1)

Finally the question is left what happens to those who until their end do not believe in Christ. Indonesian theologians who adhere to relativism would answer that the adherents of other religions can be saved also by their respective religions. Whereas the inclusivistic position would mean, that non-Christians will somehow be saved but surely by Christ. This 'universal reconciliation' based on the above cited Phil. 2:10-11 et al. was held even by some German pietistic theologians such as Johann Albrecht Bengel (1687-1752), Michael Hahn (1758–1819), Johann Heinrich Jung Stilling (1740–1817) et al., and up until the present time it is the official doctrine in many pietistic Hahnish Fellowships. Other theologians stress on the basis of Mark 16:16 etc. that "the one who does not believe will be condemned." Because

effort or merit. There is no human who is righteous before God.[a] Therefore humans can only obtain salvation by the grace and mercy of God towards man.[b]

   a. **Romans 3:10**: ... as it is written: "There is no one who is righteous, not even one; ...."– (comp. *Heidelberg Catechism*, question no. 8, no. 13-14 and no. 60-64).
   b. **Acts of the Apostles 4:12**: Salvation is found in no one else, for there is no other name under heaven given to men by which we must be saved. (*New International Version*).

Christian faith stresses that salvation can only be obtained by the life and death of / with Jesus Christ.[c] Whereas those who die outside of Christ and outside the fellowship of the believers can only be left to the authority and sovereignty of God.[d]

   c. **John 3:16**: For God so loved the world that he gave his only Son, so that everyone who believes in him may not perish but may have eternal life. (Comp. *Heidelberg Catechism*, question no. 20)
   d. **1 Corinthians 5:12-13**: For by what authority shall I judge those outside the congregation? Is it not only those who are inside the congregation that you judge? God will judge those outside the congregation. Drive out the wicked person from among you. (*Editor's translation* based on the *Indonesian official translation*, which is quite loose in this verse).

Question 23: During the encounter between different religious communities some take a fanatic attitude by humiliating or

---

the last two of the three positions described can both be based on Scripture texts the GKJTU leaves this question open, based partly on the specific Indonesian translation of 1 Cor. 5:12-13. But this does not diminish the creed of the GKJTU "that salvation can only be obtained by the life and death of Jesus Christ." Thereby the above described relativist position is rejected. The ambiguity that still remains can be partly understood because of the personal situation of many Javanese Christians. Sometimes theologians of the GKJTU say: "When we evangelize we stress those who do not believe in Christ will be eternally lost. But if I think of my many non-Christians relatives and friends I find it more difficult to utter this sentence."

In connection with this issue the formula "*extra ecclesiam nulla salus*" – "no salvation outside the Church" is very much debated. The GKJTU deliberately uses the term "the fellowship of the believers" to avoid a formalistic understanding of mere formal membership in a specific church. But for the GKJKTU belonging to that fellowship of believers is a decisive part of saving faith.

B. Realm of Religious Plurality and the Diversity of Christian Churches 47

even insulting others. One example is to call the adherents of other religions heathens. What is our attitude when we are called heathens?

The dictionary of the Indonesian language *Kamus Besar Bahasa Indonesia* explains that '*kafir*' ('*pagan*', '*heathen*') is someone who does not believe in God or in His prophet(s). Therefore the term '*kafir*' is often used to humiliate or even curse others whose conduct is not according to God's truth, or even for those of a different religion or conviction.[28] But assuming the above-mentioned basic meaning of the term, the adherents of other religions must not be called '*kafir*', including Christians. Christian faith very obviously stresses faith in God, who has worked and taken on visible form in Jesus Christ. Christians also believe in the prophets and apostles, who in a special way have received revelation from God. Through the prophets and apostles Christians understand the word of God. Thus it is not proper for anyone who acknowledges the Almighty Creator to be called '*kafir*'. Only atheists (people who deny the existence of God) with barbarian behavior can properly be called '*kafir*'.

When Christians encounter adherents of other religions who call Christians '*kafir*', Christians must not repay in the same way by calling those adherents of other religions '*kafir*'. Christian faith does not teach repaying evil with evil.[a]

a. **Matthew 5:39**: But I say to you, Do not resist an evildoer. But if anyone strikes you on the right cheek, turn the other also. – **Luke 6:29**: If anyone strikes you on the cheek, offer the other also; and from anyone who takes away your coat do not withhold even your shirt. – **1 Peter 3:9**: Do not repay evil with evil or insult with insult, but with blessing, because to this you were called so that you may inherit a blessing. (*New International Version*).

---

[28] *Translators' note:* The Arabic-Indonesian loan word '*kafir*' (from Arabic كافر – *kāfir*) actually means "someone who covers or refutes the truth." In the Quran the term is used for all those who reject the prophet Muhammad, the Quran and the exclusive belief in Allah, therefore it is also used for Christians (e.g. Surah 5, verse 17). On the other hand early Indonesian Bible Translations before 1974 also use the term '*kafir*' in verses in which some English Bible Translations use the term 'heathen' or 'pagan' (e.g. Mt 18:19). Because of its pejorative tune the term '*kafir*' is nowadays avoided among Indonesian Christians; the official Indonesian Bible translation of 1974 (and other modern Indonesian Bible translations) paraphrases the term as "those who do not know God." Also enlightened Muslims in Indonesia do not use the term '*kafir*' for the adherents of other religions, the dictionary of the Indonesian language *Kamus Besar Bahasa Indonesia* (*Comprehensive Dictionary of the Indonesian Language*) has the cautious definition cited above.

Without humiliating the adherents of other religions Christians can explain about their faith in God, the prophets and the apostles. More than that, every Christian is called to confess the faith through deeds in his or her daily life.

Question 24: In a situation of religious plurality the religious communities spread their respective religion. This can lead to conflicts among the religious communities. How does the church proclaim the Gospel in the midst of this religious plurality?

Basically every religious community has the right to spread its respective religion.[29] Every Christian has the task of proclaiming the Gospel, the good News of salvation.[a]

>   a. **Mark 16:15**: And He said to them, "Go into all the world and preach the gospel to every creature." (*New King James Version*). (Comp. *Heidelberg Catechism*, question no. 65).

Therefore evangelization is not just to make somebody change his religion. Evangelization means to scatter the seed of the Gospel by erecting the signs of the Kingdom of God.[b]

---

[29] *Translators' note:* According to the Indonesian state philosophy *Pancasila,* every Indonesian has the right and the obligation to choose freely one of the officially acknowledged high religions (or 'revealed religions'): Islam, Catholicism, Protestant Christianity, Hinduism, Buddhism or Confucianism. The traditional ethnic religions ('natural religions', 'folk religions', 'animism-dynamism') are not regarded as religions, but some of these ethnic religions have achieved status as a branch of Hinduism, e.g. the '*Kaharingan folk religion*' of the Dayak tribes in Kalimantan / Borneo. But it is forbidden to convert someone from one of the acknowledged high religions to another. Thus mission practically is only allowed among the adherents of ethnic religions ('animists'), Christian mission among e.g. Muslims is forbidden, also Muslim mission ('*da'wah*') among Christians. Indonesian Muslims call Christian mission among Muslims '*kristenisasi*' ('christianization') or '*pemurtadan*' ('making someone an apostate'). The Muslims also have their mission ('*da'wah*') among Christians, but they usually deny that and charge that only the Christians violate the laws against mission among the adherents of other religions. The Christian churches have several times complained to the government that for the adherents of all world religions (at least Christians and Muslims) the spreading of their religion is a solemn duty, which cannot be restricted by anyone, but these efforts have been futile until now. In this situation Christian evangelization must be carried out very cautiously. Above all Christian churches stress again and again that Christians are not able to 'Christianize' anyone, only the Holy Spirit can lead humans to Christian faith.

B. Realm of Religious Plurality and the Diversity of Christian Churches 49

  b. **Romans 14:17**: For the kingdom of God is not food and drink but righteousness and peace and joy in the Holy Spirit.

Therefore the Gospel is an offer, not a constraint. Thus evangelization has to be carried out wisely and politely with respect towards the other religious communities. The main task of Christians is to scatter the seed of the Gospel by serious effort and with prayer.[c] May the Lord himself make it grow. The human decision to accept the Gospel is a very private decision, brought about by the power of God.[d] The Christians are called to struggle (for it) through their witness.[e]

  c. **Mark 4:26-32**: He also said, "The kingdom of God is as if someone would scatter seed on the ground, and would sleep and rise night and day, and the seed would sprout and grow, he does not know how. The earth produces of itself, first the stalk, then the head, then the full grain in the head. But when the grain is ripe, at once he goes in with his sickle, because the harvest has come." He also said, "With what can we compare the kingdom of God, or what parable will we use for it? It is like a mustard seed, which, when sown upon the ground, is the smallest of all the seeds on earth; yet when it is sown it grows up and becomes the greatest of all shrubs, and puts forth large branches, so that the birds of the air can make nests in its shade."

  d. **John 6:44**: No one can come to me unless drawn by the Father who sent me; and I will raise that person up on the last day. – **John 6:65**: And he said, "For this reason I have told you that no one can come to me unless it is granted by the Father."

  e. **1 Timothy 4:12b**: … set the believers an example in speech and conduct, in love, in faith, in purity. (Comp. 1Peter 3:1-2).[30]

Question 25: How do the Christians work out their relationship with other religious communities?

Individual Christians and the church as a whole have to be open for dialogue and for cooperation with other religious communities.[a] This dialogue will run well if both sides meet in an atmosphere of trust and mutual respect. What should properly be discussed in this dialogue?

  a. **1 Corinthians 9:19-23**: For though I am free with respect to all, I have made myself a slave to all, so that I might win more of them. To the Jews I became as a Jew, in order to win Jews. To those under the law I became as one under the law (though I myself am not under the law) so that I might win those under the law. To those outside the law I became as one outside the law (though I am not free from God's law but am under Christ's law) so that I might win those outside

---

[30] *Translators' note:* Concerning the theme of Christian witness through good deeds more Scripture proof texts could be added: 1 Petr 2:12,15; 3:16; Phil 2:15; Mt 5:16.

the law. To the weak I became weak, so that I might win the weak. I have become all things to all people, that I might by all means save some. I do it all for the sake of the gospel, so that I may share in its blessings.

Firstly, there should be a dialogue on the life patterns and right to exist of the respective religious communities. This is very important to create an attitude of mutual respect and cooperation, so that a pattern of positive coexistence can emerge.

Secondly, there should be a dialogue about the ethics of life in order to create coexistence in dignity. Based on these two principles all religious communities can cooperate.

In this dialogue and cooperation the church and every single Christian are called to demonstrate the power, the truth and the hope which is in Christ, by exhibiting the best tangible deeds possible.[b]

> b. **Matthew 5:20**: For I tell you, unless your righteousness exceeds that of the scribes and Pharisees, you will never enter the kingdom of heaven. – **Matthew 7:12**: So whatever you wish that men would do to you, do so to them; for this is the law and the prophets. (*Revised Standard Version*).

Question 26: A society with religious plurality very easily leads to religious intermarriage. What is our view and attitude concerning this issue?

The Marriage Laws no. 1 of the year 1974 decree that a marriage is legal according to the laws of religion. That means that a marriage is legal with civil effects if it is legal according to the laws of the respective religion. As a consequence this decree forbids religious intermarriage. Nevertheless, religious intermarriage is a reality which cannot be denied in the midst of a reality of religious plurality. There are quite a lot of examples of religious intermarriage which finally were resolved by a court decision.[31] So religious intermarriage can be legalized as these precedents of jurisprudence show.

---

[31] *Translators' note:* As explained in this answer, Indonesian Law basically does not allow religious intermarriage. It is possible to get a certificate of exemption from the county court in jurisdiction, but most couples shun this option. Usually one part converts to the religion of the other to fulfill the demands of the cited law. In some cases the non-Christian part converts to a sincere, living Christian faith. In other cases the conversion is only a mere formal change of religion. In many cases Christians become Muslims because of religious intermarriage. To prevent such "forced conversions" the Indonesian churches have struggled for a long time to legalize religious intermarriage, but without much success. The Church Order of the GKJTU only allows religious intermarriage if the non-Christian party declares that he/she

B. Realm of Religious Plurality and the Diversity of Christian Churches 51

But before Christians decide on religious intermarriage they should consider the following:

Firstly, is the decision for religious intermarriage really a responsible way to create a harmonious family life?

Secondly, will the decision for religious intermarriage not have negative impacts in the future?

Thirdly, it should be considered from the aspect of faith whether religious intermarriage is really according to the will of God?[a]

> a. **2 Corinthians 6:14-16**: Do not be mismated with unbelievers. For what partnership have righteousness and iniquity? Or what fellowship has light with darkness? What accord has Christ with Belial? Or what has a believer in common with an unbeliever? What agreement has the temple of God with idols? For we are the temple of the living God; as God said, "I will live in them and move among them, and I will be their God, and they shall be my people." (*Revised Standard Version*) – **Deuteronomy 7:3-4**: Do not intermarry with them, giving your daughters to their sons or taking their daughters for your sons, for that would turn away your children from following me, to serve other gods. Then the anger of the LORD would be kindled against you, and he would destroy you quickly.

Fourthly, is religious intermarriage in accordance with the prevailing social standards, also in accordance with the traditions and teachings of the church? These four aspects should be thoroughly considered and prayed about before entering into religious intermarriage. Above all it should be kept in mind, that the ideal of God is a couple of common faith. Therefore every believer is called to bring his family to Christian faith.[b]

> b. **1 Corinthians 7:12-16**: To the rest I say – I and not the Lord – that if any believer has a wife who is an unbeliever, and she consents to live with him, he should not divorce her. And if any woman has a husband who is an unbeliever, and he consents to live with her, she should not divorce him. For the unbelieving husband is made holy through his wife, and the unbelieving wife is made holy through her husband. Otherwise, your children would be unclean, but as it is, they are holy. But if the unbelieving partner separates, let it be so; in such a case the brother or sister is not bound. It is to peace that God has called you. Wife,
>
> will not hinder the activities of Christian faith of the Christian spouse nor prevent the baptism and Christian education of their children. As this answer (with all its Javanese indirectness) shows, the GKJTU basically rejects religious intermarriage – except the non-Christian partner converts to a sincere Christian faith before the wedding takes place, so that the marriage actually is no longer interreligious. For many Christian parents in Indonesia it is one the most important prayers that their children will get a (Protestant) Christian spouse.

for all you know, you might save your husband. Husband, for all you know, you might save your wife.

Question 27: It may happen that adherents of different religions meet and pray together for the issues they face together. What is our view and attitude concerning this phenomenon?

In every religion people pray as a means to sustain the relationship of their religious community with God. Facing common problems it can easily happen that people pray together although they belong to different religious communities.[32] Christian faith or respectively the church does not forbid its members to attend such interreligious prayers. Nevertheless Christians have to preserve their Christian identity during such prayers, because Christian prayers have their own special characteristics.[a] If the prayer is led by a non-Christian, the Christian must say their own, silent Christian prayer. But if in certain circumstances Christians are asked to lead the prayer they should say a Christian prayer and give opportunity to present adherents of other religions to say a silent prayer according to their religious conviction. Thus the Christians can show their solidarity with other people through their prayers.

   a. **John 14:13**: I will do whatever you ask in my name, so that the Father may be glorified in the Son. (Comp. *Heidelberg Catechism*, question no. 117-120).

---

[32] ***Translators' note:*** According to the *Pancasila* state philosophy (ideology) all Indonesians (have to) believe in God. Therefore common prayers are a standard part of most public meetings. Usually those attending are asked for a given time to utter a silent prayer according to their respective religion. Nowadays this silent prayer often is followed by a prayer lead aloud by a Muslim prayer leader. At neighborhood or village meetings sometimes Christians might be asked to lead this common prayer (in some cases they might even be asked to give a devotional message). Usually the Christians gratefully accept this missionary opportunity and say a Christian prayer. Such a specific Christian prayer is characterized as a prayer to God the Father, uses the formula 'in Jesus name' (see the cited Scripture from John 14:13-14, also 16:23-26), but also mentions specific points of Christian faith, such as the 'love of God', 'atonement', 'grace' etc. During such an interreligious prayer wise Christians will use these specific Christian terms in a well-balanced proportion. But over cautious Christians might even totally avoid any specifically Christian vocabulary in such a situation and just say a 'commonly religious' prayer. Nevertheless before saying a Christian prayer the Christians usually will apologize to the adherents of other religions – whereas most Muslim prayer leader do not deem it necessary to apologize to the adherents of other religions. At meetings of interreligious dialogue interreligious prayers also are used, but such meetings are much scarcer than those organized by institutions of the government or of the society.

B. Realm of Religious Plurality and the Diversity of Christian Churches

Question 28: Within Christianity there is also a plurality. What is our attitude when working out our relationship with diverse kinds of Christian movements and denominations?

Obviously the churches in Indonesia are quite diverse. This situation can be roughly described as follows:

Firstly there is the Catholic Church which is organizationally one.

Secondly we have the churches stemming from the Reformation, i.e. the Lutheran, Calvinist and Mennonite churches.

Thirdly there are churches which came up after the Reformation, such as the Baptist, Methodist, Pentecostal, Adventist etc. churches. Besides that there are what we call movements within the churches, such as the Charismatic Movement, Toronto Blessing etc. There are also cults who have segregated themselves from the Christian churches, who deny basic Christian doctrines but regard themselves as the only true Church. Among these are the Children of God, the Mormons and Jehovah's Witnesses. There is even the 'Church of Satan' which is clearly outside Christianity.

So what is the attitude of the Christians / the GKJTU towards this plurality?

Firstly, this variety of church denominations is accepted as a reality in the sense that this variety is a proper way of humans to relate to God. This variety should be understood as a way God uses because He wants to reach and minister all humans in their different contexts. It also can be understood as a way of humans to respond to the message of salvation according to their surrounding context. That means that all the churches with all their differences are basically one, they are one in their faith in Christ.[a]

> a. **1 Corinthians 12:12-14**: For just as the body is one and has many members, and all the members of the body, though many, are one body, so it is with Christ. For in the one Spirit we were all baptized into one body ... and we were all made to drink of one Spirit. Indeed, the body does not consist of one member but of many.

Yet we can apply this acknowledgement and esteem only to those churches which confess the Lord Jesus Christ as God and Savior according to the scriptures, and seek to fulfill together their common calling to the glory of the one God, Father, Son and Holy Spirit.[33] If there is a church or Christian movement which is in contrast to that basis, than we have to reject it firmly.[b]

---

[33] *Translators' note:* This answer first quotes the basis of the World Council of Churches from 1961 as the 'least common denominator' of all Christian churches: "(The World Council of Churches is a fellowship of) churches which confess the

b. **Ephesians 4:14-15**: We must no longer be children, tossed to and fro and blown about by every wind of doctrine, by people's trickery, by their craftiness in deceitful scheming. But speaking the truth in love, we must grow up in every way into him who is the head, into Christ. – **2 John 1:7-11**: Many deceivers have gone out into the world, those who do not confess that Jesus Christ has come in the flesh; any such person is the deceiver and the antichrist! Be on your guard, so that you do not lose what we have worked for, but may receive a full reward. Everyone who does not abide in the teaching of Christ, but goes beyond it, does not have God; whoever abides in the teaching has both the Father and the Son. Do not receive into the house or welcome anyone who comes to you and does not bring this teaching; for to welcome is to participate in the evil deeds of such a person.

Secondly, identity has to be safeguarded in the midst of that variety. All churches who believe in Christ as Lord and Savior have to be acknowledged and respected. But that does not mean that Christians / the GKJTU regard all churches as the same. Every church has its unique specifics, according to its surrounding context. Every Christian is bound to such a specific fellowship. Therefore it cannot be justified if a Christians moves from church to

---

Lord Jesus Christ as God and Savior according to the scriptures, and (therefore) seek to fulfill together their common calling to the glory of the one God, Father, Son and Holy Spirit." In line with Javanese tolerance, all other doctrinal differences of the churches are regarded as caused by 'different surrounding contexts' only. Also the unique identity of the GKJTU is caused by its specific context. This unique identity of the GKJTU comprises characteristics as e.g. its pietistic piety, its reformed liturgy with reformed and pietistic hymns, the Heidelberg Catechism with its Update as the basic doctrine of the GKJTU, infant baptism by sprinkling, its presbyterial-synodal church order, its usage of the Javanese language during the services, its occasional usage of Javanese traditional fine arts etc. To some extent the GKJTU has deliberately decided on these characteristics, but other characteristics are really more or less historical coincidence, caused by the 'surrounding context' of the GKJTU.

This answer of the Catechism-Update calls the members of the GKJTU to be loyal towards their church and its characteristics. The members of the GKJTU are usually very loyal to their home congregation, but when moving to another town the members of the GKJTU (like the members of many other churches) very easily join a very different (charismatic) church, without regard to whether there is a GKJTU congregation or a congregation of a similar church in that town. This phenomena is partly caused by the fact that compared to many GKJTU congregations (and other protestant congregations), charismatic and Pentecostal congregations are much more eager to go after those who have newly moved in. When coming back to their home congregation these (former) GKJTU members sometimes try to reshape that congregation according to the identity of their new church. Therefore the GKJTU strives to teach the church members about its own identity through seminars and this very Catechism-Update. The GKJTU tries to lead the church members towards a better understanding of the identity of the GKJTU as a whole.

B. Realm of Religious Plurality and the Diversity of Christian Churches 55

church. Changing church membership even once has to be based on appropriate reasons.

The GKJTU has a unique identity which cannot be found in other churches, although they all believe in Christ as Lord and Savior. Therefore all members of the GKJTU should properly take care of and build up their church as a place where they can praise God for that salvation and work it out in their lives. Every Christian fellowship needs such a faithful attitude. Faithfully to build up the fellowship within the GKJTU is therefore the calling of every member of the GKJTU.

Question 29: To live within a context of church variety makes it possible to attend the meetings of other churches. What is our view and attitude concerning attendance at the meetings of other churches?

Christians have to be open, but also critical in order to safeguard the identity of their church. But this should not be misunderstood as if safeguarding the identity means to shut oneself off. Especially the GKJTU has to be open towards the ongoing developments of Christianity. To be open means to be ready to understand and even to receive, on the basis of mature consideration and investigation.[34] Thereby the GKJTU can receive but also reject something on the basis of considerations of theological responsibility. Everything

---

[34] ***Translators' note:*** This answer has to be understood on the background of negative experiences of the GKJTU (and other churches) with charismatic and Pentecostal churches, which are very active in Salatiga and the surrounding area, in the city of Semarang, but also in the rest of the area of the GKJTU. Those charismatic and Pentecostal churches invite the members of the GKJTU for evangelistic meetings, seminars etc., offer attractive facilities (pick up service, free lunch etc.) until those invited finally become members of their church. On the one hand, many poor GKJTU members feel much honored when e.g. picked up by car; on the other hand many GKJTU congregations lack the resources to offer such services. The much more lively church services and the very practically orientated preaching of the charismatic churches also attract the members of GKJTU. Also when village congregations split (because of family conflicts etc.) the charismatic churches receive the split off group with open arms to found a rival congregation in the respective village. The charismatic churches entice members even from one another. Therefore the GKJTU is very open for cooperation within the 'Communion of Churches of Indonesia' (PGI), has manifold international ecumenical contacts, but is very cautious with cooperation with charismatic or Pentecostal groups. But there are also cases of positive cooperation with charismatic and evangelical groups, especially within the local forums of cooperation between Christian churches, which consist of Roman Catholic and Protestant as well as charismatic and Pentecostal churches. E.g. every

has to be thoroughly tested against the truth of the Word of God. To be open includes also the readiness for cooperation in order to tighten the fellowship and work out an even deeper togetherness. But the GKJTU also has to be critical towards all invitations for cooperation: Is it really about cooperation only? Or is there some hidden agenda? Cooperation should not become a disguise which ends up in 'sheep stealing' from other churches.

To be critical thus means to be full of understanding but to consider the truth. On this basis the GKJTU can accept some things, reject others partly or even wholly if it is clearly in contrast to the truth of the Word of God.

---

year all churches of Salatiga organize a common service at Christmas, Easter and Pentecost, in which the GKJTU is actively involved.

Unfortunately this answer still lacks Scripture proof texts, such as e.g.: "test everything; hold fast to what is good" (1 Thess. 5:21; comp. also Acts 17:11).

C. Realm of Politics

Question 30: What is the meaning of the term 'politics'?

The term 'politics' stems from the Greek word *'polis'* which means 'city' or 'state', also from the word *'politeia'* meaning citizenry, citizenship, state constitution and state order.[35] According to that basic meaning, the word 'politics' can be explained as follows:

Firstly, it is the art or science of government or of the state, such as the state system or the principles of government.

Secondly politics comprise political actions and policies (strategies and policies to achieve something) both in home affairs and in foreign affairs.

Thirdly, it can mean ways of conduct or policies to face and handle a certain affair.[36]

As a conclusion, politics is the science about and all actions concerning decision-making in a system of society (e.g. a state) which result in regulations and their implication for the common welfare.

Question 31: What then is the state?

Basically the state is a social system under control of a certain geographical area, organized under a political body, i.e. a sovereign and legitimate government, respected by the people, in order to achieve the form of common life desired. Thus the state, comprising both the government and the people, achieves its goal based on the order agreed together. As an organization the

---

[35] *Translators' note:* Usually the term 'politics' is derived from the Greek words *'politikos'* (anything concerning the state or city affairs), *'politike techne'* ('the art, science or technique of government'), *'polites'* ('citizen'), *'politeia'* ('citizenry', 'citizenship', 'state constitution', 'state order') and *'polis'* ('city', 'state'). To simplify matters, the GKJTU Appendix mentions only the last two Greek terms in the etymological part of its answer.

[36] *Kamus Besar Bahasa Indonesia* (*Comprehensive Dictionary of the Indonesian Language*), 3rd edition, page 886.

state has the task of ordering power[37] so that it can become an effective tool in order to bring about the common goal.[38]

Question 32: The state is an organization or institution that exercises power. So what is that state power all about?

The power or authority of the state is an institutionalized and organized power as a means to run the state. Therefore this state power requires responsibility from the side of those in power and loyalty of those under their power.

Question 33: Who exercises this state authority?

The body which runs the authority of the state is called government. So what is the government?[39]

Firstly it is a system to run the authority and power to order the social, economic and political life of a state or part of a state.

Secondly, the government is understood as the ruler of a state or part of a state.

---

[37] *Translators' note:* The Indonesian text of question 31-45 again and again mentions the terms '*kuasa*' and '*kekuasaan*', which are both usually translated as 'power', 'supremacy', 'dominion' or 'authority' – which sometimes have a negative tone to the Western reader. Also the Indonesian people often have experienced state power as arbitrary and corrupt during the 32-year dictatorship of Suharto and also in other eras and areas. Therefore the GKJTU-Update tries to underline the basically positive value of an ordered state authority. This English translation renders the Indonesian words '*kuasa*' and '*kekuasaan*' by the terms 'power', 'authority' or 'dominion', according to its context.

[38] *Kamus Besar Bahasa Indonesia* (*Comprehensive Dictionary of the Indonesian Language*), 3rd edition, page 77.

[39] *Translators' note:* The Suharto regime always tried to identify the interests of the state and the interests of the Suharto government. Therefore the terms 'state' ('*negara*') and 'government' ('*pemerintah*') were and are used almost interchangeable in modern Indonesian; e.g. state property is often called government property (a phenomena which also occurs in other languages). Besides that the Suharto regime feigned legitimacy by manipulated elections. Therefore it was deemed necessary to stress again and again that the Suharto regime was a legitimate government and any form of opposition was regarded as resistance against the legitimate government. That is why the GKJTU-Update regards it as very necessary to give a clear definition and biblical understanding of the terms 'state', 'government' and 'legitimate government'.

C. Realm of Politics

Fourthly it can mean the highest body which governs a state, e.g. the president and his cabinet.[40]

Question 34: Every government holds and executes authority. Where does this authority originate from?

The power and authority of the state can originate from different sources, depending on the form of government and the ideology to which that state adheres. Basically there are three sources of state authority:

Firstly, state authority from religious sources, i.e. state authority is derived from the conviction that a super human power, i.e. God, who gives the state the right to rule and govern its people.[a]

> a. **Genesis 1:28**: God blessed them, and God said to them, "Be fruitful and multiply, and fill the earth and subdue it; and have dominion over the fish of the sea and over the birds of the air and over every living thing that moves upon the earth."

Secondly, state authority may be defined in an elitist understanding, based on the conviction that a certain group within the state has extraordinary abilities, which entitles them to rule and govern the others. Such groups might be the aristocrats (the noblemen), the military, the technocrats or those who adhere most faithfully to the state ideology.

Thirdly, state authority can be understood democratically, i.e. state authority is based on the conviction, that popular sovereignty gives the right to rule and to govern the state,[41] according to a well-known slogan of democracy: "Of the People, By the People, For the People".

---

[40] *Kamus Besar Bahasa Indonesia* (*Comprehensive Dictionary of the Indonesian Language*), 3rd edition, page 859.

[41] **Translators' note:** Popular sovereignty is clearly rooted in the Indonesian Constitution. In its preamble it is stated: "The Republic of Indonesia is based on popular sovereignty", than it goes on in article 1, paragraph 2: "Sovereignty is in the hands of the people and is executed according to the Constitution." Of course it is impossible to discuss all the problems of direct democracy and supremacy of human rights above popular sovereignty in this short Catechism-Update. Even the 'Guided Democracy' of Sukarno and the 'New Order' of Dictator Suharto were feigned as forms of popular sovereignty. The cited definition of democracy as "government of the people, by the people, for the people" was coined by US President Abraham Lincoln in his *Gettysburg Address* in 1863.

Question 35: Which of these three sources of state authority are according to the Bible?

Basically every human has been given dominion from God.[42] Therefore Christian faith holds it that all authority, whatever its source may be, originates from God who has given the mandate to take care of the whole creation.[a] Therefore all forms of power have to be received with thanksgiving and responsibility as a grace of God.[b]

  a. **Genesis 1:28**: God blessed them, and God said to them, "Be fruitful and multiply, and fill the earth and subdue it; and have dominion over the fish of the sea and over the birds of the air and over every living thing that moves upon the earth." – **John 19:10-11**: Then Pilate said to Him, "Are You not speaking to me? Do You not know that I have power to crucify You, and power to release You?" Jesus answered, "You could have no power at all against Me unless it had been given you from above. Therefore the one who delivered Me to you has the greater sin." (*New King James Version*).

  b. **Proverbs 28:28**: When the wicked rise to power, people go into hiding; but when the wicked perish, the righteous thrive. (*New International Version*).

Question 36: Why does the Bible teach that the power of the state has to be received as a grace of God?

Every power given to a human, however little it may be is a gift of God. God has a purpose when giving power to humans. That power is the 'arm of God' to order and shape human life so that it will be more civilized. In other words, God rules and governs the world through humans, so that life with peace and welfare can come about. Therefore it is proper to call whatever government a servant of God, because it is the duty of every government to serve the will of God in this world. To execute that duty the government is given power to use the 'sword of power' to execute God's wrath on the wrongdoers.[a] That means that the government is given authority and power to act severely, defend and maintain justice and combat crime.

  a. **Romans 13:4**: for it is God's servant for your good. But if you do what is wrong, you should be afraid, for the authority does not bear the sword in vain! It is the servant of God to execute wrath on the wrongdoer. (Comp. *Heidelberg Catechism*, question no. 105 and no. 110).

---

[42] *Translators' note:* In this answer the source of all power is based on the creational mandate according to Genesis 1:28. Of course, other Biblical references could be cited also to show that all sovereigns have received their power from God, such as Daniel 2:21, Proverbs 21:1, Romans 13:1 etc.

C. Realm of Politics

After the fall humans are indeed prone to hate God and fellow humans,[b] which than leads to devastating deeds. But through a good government God works to erect virtue and combat evil. The task of the government is to work out this mission of God in this world. A government which departs from this mission of God will fail and mankind will be ruled by unrighteousness.

> b. **Romans 3:23-24**: all have sinned and are deprived of the glory of God. They are justified freely by his grace through the redemption in Christ Jesus. (*New American Bible*). – **Psalm 36:2**: Transgression speaks to the wicked deep in their hearts; there is no fear of God before their eyes. – **Psalm 14:1b-3**: Fools say in their hearts, "There is no God." They are corrupt, they do abominable deeds; there is no one who does well. The LORD looks down from heaven on humankind to see if there are any who are wise, who seek after God. They have all gone astray, they are all alike perverse; there is no one who does good, no, not one. (Comp. *Heidelberg Catechism*, question no. 8).

Question 37: The Bible has the understanding that the power of the state is a gift of God. So what is then the attitude of the Christians towards state and government?

Christians are obliged to respect and obey the government and the state,[a] as good citizens who are obedient to the government and in harmony with their fellow citizens. This attitude of obedience towards the state and the government is obligatory at all levels of government, from the highest to the lowest.[b]

> a. **Matthew 22:18-21**: Jesus … said, " … Show me the coin used for the tax." And they brought him a denarius. Then he said to them, "Whose head is this, and whose title?" They answered, "The emperor's." Then he said to them, "Give therefore to the emperor the things that are the emperor's, and to God the things that are God's."
>
> b. **1 Peter 2:13-14**: For the Lord's sake accept the authority of every human institution, whether of the emperor as supreme, or of governors, as sent by him to punish those who do wrong and to praise those who do right. – **Romans 13:1-2.5**: Let every person be subject to the governing authorities; for there is no authority except from God, and those authorities that exist have been instituted by God. Therefore whoever resists authority resists what God has appointed, and those who resist will incur judgment. … Therefore one must be subject, not only because of wrath but also because of conscience.

This obedience of the Christians towards the state and the government however is not a slavish obedience, obeying whatever the government demands. The obedience of the Christians towards the state is conditioned by righteousness and truth.

Question 38: What conditions have to be fulfilled by a state and a government to be respected and obeyed by the Christians and the other citizens?

Firstly, state and government have to be able to maintain law and order in justice.

Secondly, state and government are obliged to honor the basic rights of every citizen such as the right to life and liberty, the right to participate in the political life by electing and being elected, the right to practice a freely chosen religion, the right to education, the right to work, just legal treatment etc.[43] The state and the government have to guarantee the human rights of every citizen in order to bring about peaceful and civilized co-existence.

Thirdly, state and government are obliged to treat every citizen equally, without different treatment based on ethnicity, religion, race, party membership, culture, income, education etc., also to safeguard the integrity of creation. On this basis the state and the government are obliged to bring out the common welfare, not just the welfare of a certain group within the society. State and government have to treat all citizens equally.[a]

> a. **Proverbs 29:4:** By justice a king gives stability to the land; but he who imposes heavy taxes ruins it. (*New American Bible*). (Comp. also Genesis 1:28).

Question 39: What can Christians as fellow citizens do if the state does not fulfill the above-mentioned conditions?

If the state does not guarantee the welfare of its citizens, acts arbitrarily, violates human rights, issues unjust decrees etc. Christians are allowed to not obey those decisions which are contrary to the truth of the Word of God. Christians have to obey the Word of God rather than an unjust state or an unjust government.[a]

---

[43] ***Translators' note:*** The human rights mentioned here are more or less according to those mentioned in the Indonesian Constitution, only the right to freely choose a religion is not so explicitly mentioned there, the *Indonesian Constitution*, Art. 29.2, only mentions the "freedom of every citizen to embrace and practice his religion." But of course for the sake of evangelization the right to freely choose or change one's religion is very important to the GKJTU. The formula "without difference of ethnicity, religion, race and party membership" is often used in discussions about civil and human rights in Indonesia and within the Catechism-Update, but the rejection of sexual discrimination is characteristically absent.

C. Realm of Politics

a. **Acts of the Apostles 5:29**: But Peter and the apostles answered, "We must obey God rather than men." (*Revised Standard Version*).

Christians even have to be courageous in struggling for the truth and uttering it in a proper way in order to make a path for renewal so that the state and the government comes back to the way of righteousness and truth.[44] Christians fulfill that task out of respect and love towards the state which basically is only in place by the grace of God.

Question 40: What is necessary for the state to fulfill its function properly?

The state needs a governing body which holds and executes the state's authority. This comprises the following elements:

Firstly, the state needs state rules which are included in a legal constitution (a legal system consisting of laws, regulations, prescriptions etc.). These regulations have three functions, i.e. to regulate the relationship between the governing bodies, also the relationship between the governing bodies and the citizens and finally between the citizens themselves. Thus these regulations form a commonly agreed set of rules in order to achieve an ideal condition toward which people aspire together. To bring these regulations into effective function, all parties have to follow them, both the governing bodies as well as the citizens.[a]

a. **2 Timothy 1:7**: For God gave us not a spirit of fearfulness; but of power and love and discipline. (*American Standard Version*). (Comp. *GKJTU-Update of the Heidelberg Catechism*, question no. 32 above).

Secondly, the state needs guardians and upholders of law and order. These have the task of watching over the implementation of the above-mentioned rules (the law and all legal regulations) to be kept properly. They also have the task to proceed against and punish any offender according to legal procedures.[b]

b. **Ezra 7:26**: All who will not obey the law of your God and the law of the king, let judgment be strictly executed on them, whether for death or for banishment or for confiscation of their goods or for imprisonment. – **Proverbs 20:26**: A wise king winnows the wicked, and drives the wheel over them.

---

[44] Comp. *GKJTU-Update of the Heidelberg Catechism*, question no. 41 below.

Thirdly, the state needs the active participation of its citizens to make the governing bodies function. Every good citizen is called to be actively involved in government by using his electoral rights, support the programs of the government, fulfilling its controlling function etc.

Question 41: Why does the law also have to be applied to those in power and why is it necessary to guard and control those in power?

The worldwide history of the states proves that those in power are prone to misuse their power, practice corruption and act arbitrarily. It even can be said: The bigger the power of a state or a government, the bigger the risk of its misuse. Theologically spoken, those in power are sinful humans who are always prone to sin.[a] Their sin takes the shape of misuse of power for the interest of themselves, of their families, their group or class. Thereby they also act arbitrarily towards others.

> a. **Romans 3:9-10**: What then? Are we any better off? No, not at all; for we have already charged that all, both Jews and Greeks, are under the power of sin, as it is written: "There is no one who is righteous, not even one;" (Comp. *Heidelberg Catechism*, question no. 9).

Therefore the state power has to be limited, controlled and ordered, so that the state power can become a positive means for the peace and welfare of society. In order that the state power is used according to the law, all elements of society have to play an active part to guard and control the usage of the state power according to the democratic mechanism agreed upon.

Question 42: In what ways do Christians participate in the life of the state?

Basically every citizen has the responsibility to make a positive contribution towards the life of the state. Christians as 'God's chosen people' are under duty to become good examples and pioneers when executing their civil duties. So Christians have a fivefold role within civil life.[45]

---

[45] ***Translators' note:*** The Indonesian general and lay theologian T.B. Simatupang in 1964 coined the formula that the churches and Christians should play a "positive, creative, critical and realistic" role within the Indonesian Pancasila state (comp. Jan Sihar Aritonang and Karel Steenbrink (Eds.) *A History of Christianity in Indonesia*, Leiden: Brill, 2008, p. 780) – although Indonesian churches seldom took a critical

C. Realm of Politics

Firstly they have a **participatory role**, i.e. Christians use their rights and their obligations responsibly to build up good social and civil life.[a]

> a. **Jeremiah 29:7**: Work for the good of the city to which I have exiled you; pray to Yahweh on its behalf, since on its welfare yours depends. (*New Jerusalem Bible*).

Secondly they have a **critical and prophetical role**, i.e. Christians have to raise their critical, positive and creative prophetic voice boldly. In detail this can mean any support to uphold the laws,[46] defend justice, fight against corruption, also to critique the policies and regulations of the government or laws that deviate from the Constitution or are in favor of only a certain group of the society.[b]

> b. **Jeremiah 7:1-7**: The word that came to Jeremiah from the LORD: Stand in the gate of the LORD's house, and proclaim there this word, and say, Hear the word of the LORD, ... if you truly act justly one with another, if you do not oppress the alien, the orphan, and the widow, or shed innocent blood in this place, ... then I will dwell with you in this place, in the land that I gave of old to your ancestors forever and ever.

Thirdly they have a **mediatory role**, i.e. Christians are under the obligation to pray for the state and its government that it will act according to the laws and according to the will of God.[c]

> c. **1 Timothy 2:1-2**: First of all, then, I urge that supplications, prayers, intercessions, and thanksgivings be made for everyone, for kings and all who are in high positions, so that we may lead a quiet and peaceable life in all godliness and dignity.

---

stand towards the Suharto regime 1966-1998. During the discussion about Simatupang's formula it was modified becoming "participatory-critical-prophetical-mediatory-transforming-reforming".

[46] ***Translators' note:*** Some fundamentalist Islamic groups are trying to introduce the Islamic *Sharia*-Law bit by bit, again and again promoting bills in the spirit of the *Sharia*. In some provinces and districts Muslim fundamentalist governors and leading officials can make local regulations in the spirit of the *Sharia* or even prepare the official implementation of the *Sharia* for that area. On the other hand many good Indonesian state laws are not implemented because of the ignorance of the people or even the authorities, because the authorities deliberately leave the people in ignorance or because the people do not dare to claim their rights. Therefore Christians have to help to "uphold the laws" and "critique the policies and regulations of the government or laws that ... are in favor of only a certain group of the society". So the GKJTU again and again has organized seminars to enlighten the members of their congregations and the rest of the community about their rights and about legal bills being discussed.

Fourthly they have a **transforming role**, i.e. Christians should responsibly help to transform (change) the social life according to the values of truth, justice, honesty and faithfulness. This role and vocation also intrinsically includes the field of politics, so that even political life becomes true, just, honest and faithful.

Fifthly they have a **reforming role**, i.e. Christians must be ready to constantly renew themselves and society.^d

> d. **Romans 12:2**: Do not be conformed to this world, but be transformed by the renewing of your minds, so that you may discern what is the will of God – what is good and acceptable and perfect. (Comp. *Heidelberg Catechism*, question no. 45 and 89).

Question 43: Everything explained thus far is about the relationship of the state or politics with the people. So how about the relationship of the church towards the state and towards politics?

The Church is an independent community of its own kind, different from political or civil communities. Although the Church exists and lives in the midst of the political community, the Church is not identical with any political community. Theologically speaking, the Church is not of the world, although the Church lives within and for the world.[47] Whereas politics are of the world as a means to shape the common life in this world. The attitude of Christians concerning the relationship of Church and state is based on the attitude of the Lord Jesus when tested by the Pharisees concerning the question whether it was lawful to pay taxes to the emperor. Jesus answered that "the things that are the emperor's" should be given to the emperor, and "to God the things that are God's."^a

> a. **Matthew 22:21b**: Then he said to them, "Give therefore to the emperor the things that are the emperor's, and to God the things that are God's."

Jesus' answer makes clear that the political power is limited to the life outside the Church. Whereas life within the Church is ruled and governed by the Lord Jesus alone. Church and state are two different realms. Politics or the state are not allowed to meddle in the affairs of the Church. Politics may not turn the Church into a part of the state. Also vice versa: The Church is not allowed to meddle with political affairs. The Church is not allowed to make the state into a part of the Church. But this does not mean that Church

---

[47] *Translators' note:* This passage implicitly cites John 17:14-16 (and 1 John 2:2) although these verses are not explicitly quoted.

C. Realm of Politics

and state are completely separate and have nothing to do with each other. The Church is indeed different from the state, Church and state have different tasks. Nevertheless, the two can relate, cooperate and supplement each other. The Church can give assistance and input to the civil authorities. On the other hand, the state safeguards the security of the Church.[48]

Question 44: So what does the cooperation of politics / the state and the Church actually look like?

The state has the obligation to safeguard justice, peace and tranquility. Therefore it is just proper that the state safeguards the religious life for all adherents of any religion, including safety for the Christian Church. That means the state has to safeguard the right to worship for the adherents of all the different religions.[a]

> a. **Romans 13:13-14**: let us live honorably as in the day, not in reveling and drunkenness, not in debauchery and licentiousness, not in quarreling and jealousy. Instead, put on the Lord Jesus Christ, and make no provision for the flesh, to gratify its desires.

Whereas the Church can actively support the civil authorities through her prayer for the government, by advice and by obedience towards the government, as far as the rules of the government are not against the will of God.[b]

> b. **Psalm 72:1-2; 11-12**: Give the king your justice, O God, and your righteousness to a king's son. May he judge your people with righteousness, and your poor

---

[48] *Translators' note:* The reformational GKJTU tries to make a synthesis of the Lutheran 'two kingdoms' teaching, the Calvinist theocracy concept and the concrete situation of Church and state within the Pancasila-state of Indonesia. The Pancasila-state philosophy (or 'ideology') tries to find a middle way between a state religion and a secularized state. No single religion is declared as state religion, but all recognized religions (Islam, Christianity, Hinduism, Buddhism, and Confucianism) are equally supported. Therefore all recognized religious communities have e.g. an advisory role within the Indonesian parliament; on the other hand the authorities have the duty to protect all recognized religious communities. Nevertheless the Muslims are granted special privileges because of their majority status. After the bloody conflicts on the Moluccas (1999-2002) and in Central Sulawesi (1998-2001) the security forces often shy away from severe measures against violent Islamic fundamentalists. Destruction of churches etc. is tolerated with the argument that further civil war has to be avoided. Only the bomb attacks of Islamic terrorists in Indonesia (since 2002) and the attacks against moderate Muslim clergymen by fundamentalists have opened the eyes of the public a little bit about the dangers from the side of the fundamentalists.

with justice. ... May all kings fall down before him, all nations give him service. For he delivers the needy when they call, the poor and those who have no helper.

Question 45: May the church be active in politics?

Every church exists and lives in a certain state. Therefore this church cannot be separated from that political context. Every church is rather called to take an active role to build up a positive political climate. In this sense every church has to become salt and light for the world of politics,[49] in the framework of the threefold calling of the Church[50] for fellowship,[a] witness[b] and service.[c]

- a. **Hebrews 10:25**: We should not stay away from our assembly, as is the custom of some, but encourage one another, and this all the more as you see the day drawing near. (*New American Bible*).
- b. **Matthew 28:19-20**: Go therefore and make disciples of all nations, baptizing them in the name of the Father and of the Son and of the Holy Spirit, and teaching them to obey everything that I have commanded you. And remember, I am with you always, to the end of the age.
- c. **Romans 12:11**: Do not lag in zeal, be ardent in spirit, serve the Lord.

But if politics are understood as the struggle of groups and party to gain state power for certain groupings, than a church is not allowed to be engaged in practical politics. A church must not be affiliated with any political party or political group. The church has to be independent and free to struggle for different aspirations for the sake of a better society and state. Christ's mandate in the field of politics should be fulfilled by struggling for justice, welfare, humanity and integrity of creation (ecology). The church has to be neutral, not siding with any class, group or part of society.

---

[49] *Translators' note:* Of course this phrase implicitly cites Mt 5:13-16, a text very important for the contemporary understanding of mission in Indonesia – even though those verses are not explicitly cited here.

[50] *Translators' note:* The threefold calling of the Church as '*koinonia*' – '*martyria*' – '*diakonia*' i.e. 'fellowship' – 'witness' – 'service' has been formulated as an essential part of the Constitution of the World Council of Churches from its founding in 1948 until today. Since then it has become a common formula of the churches throughout the world. Especially in Indonesia it is used by Christians from all kinds of theological backgrounds. For the further usage of this formula within the Catechism-Update, comp. question 54 below.

C. Realm of Politics

Question 46: So how about the calling of the Church to proclaim the mandate of Christ in all aspects of life? Is the realm of politics an exception?

Of course not. The Church always has to proclaim the mandate of Christ in all aspects of life, including the realm of politics. Nevertheless, when a church proclaims the mandate of Christ in the realm of politics, the church should not only strive for the interests of the church or of the Christians, but for the common interests. The mandate of Christ in the realm of politics is being proclaimed through the struggle for justice, truth and welfare for all, without distinguishing according to ethnicity, religion, color of skin, class, social and economical status, party membership etc.[51] The church has to be neutral, not siding with any class, group or parts of the society.[52]

Question 47: How can the independence and freedom of the church with regard to politics and state affairs be safeguarded?

Basically the church may not become a political arena. Christians must not use their church as a political instrument or a political basis. In this matter church officials play an important role. Therefore church officials are not allowed to hold a political office at the same time.[53] They can only do so if

---

[51] *Translators' note:* In this context the Indonesian text several times uses the term "to proclaim the mandate of Christ", because the GKJTU understands its political actions as a part of its holistic mission. Nevertheless it is not a verbal proclamation that is primarily in mind but rather actions. Therefore the term could also be translated as "to fulfill the mandate of Christ". The GKJTU fulfills that mandate mainly by seminars on political and legal mandates, to which members of all religious and social groups are invited. Other Indonesian churches and Christian groups also offer legal aid and advocacy for those deprived of their rights, Christian newspapers publish such cases of injustice.

[52] *Translators' note:* This last sentence of answer no. 45 and 46 looks like a duplication. But answer 45 implies primarily neutrality towards political parties, answer 46 stresses that Christians should struggle for the whole community and not only for their own religious community, church or ethnic group.

[53] *Translators' note:* According to its Presbyterian order, the GKJTU actually acknowledges three special church offices (besides the universal priesthood of all believers): the diaconate, the presbyterate and the office of the 'teaching elder', which is held by the pastors and evangelists. But this regulation is actually meant for the pastors and evangelists only. 'Political offices' are here understood as offices connected with the membership in a specific party, e.g. member of a parliament. The GKJTU does not object if presbyters or deacons are engaged in a political party or if pastors or evangelists hold an office as a mayor in their village.

they step down from their church office first, so that they are active in politics not as church officials but as ordinary citizens.

D. Realm of Economy

Question 48: What is meant by 'economy' and 'business'?[54]

The term 'economy' stems from the Greek word '*oikonomia*', '*oikos*' meaning 'house', 'world'[55] or 'dwelling', whereas '*nomos*' means 'law', 'decree', 'habit' or 'order'. The verb '*nemeo*' means 'to order', 'to manage', 'to steward', so that '*oikonomeo*' means to 'manage a household'. Thus economy can be understood as the management of household affairs. This management has the aim that all resources in that household, such as food, are supplied sufficiently so that life and welfare are guaranteed. In a wider sense, economy is not restricted to household affairs.

First, economy / economics a social science concerned chiefly with the principles of production, distribution, and consumption of goods and assets, with branches such as money economy, industry and trade.

Secondly, economy refers to the use of money, human resources, time etc.[56] Thus economy is not only restricted to household affairs, but comprises the whole world. By economy the world is managed and organized by humans in order to become a comfortable place to live, and capable of supplying the necessities of human life. In brief, economy is the effort of humans both in their private households as well as in a wider sense, to provide the necessities of life in order to achieve welfare.

Whereas business is a commercial enterprise in the field of trade.[57] Business actually is a part of economic activity, but it is more directly aimed towards efforts to gain profit. For the sake of gaining that profit business efforts often even forsake ethics and morals. So the difference between economy and

---

[54] *Translators' note:* The Greek loan word '*ekonomi*' and the English loan word '*bisnis*' is quite frequently used in Indonesian, but the Indonesian term '*ekonomi*' comprises both 'economy' and 'economics'. The Catechism-Update very much stresses the meaning of the term '*oikonomia*' in Biblical Greek, over against the modern use of the term 'economy' in English or '*ekonomi*' in Indonesian.

[55] *Translators' note:* For the Greek term '*oikos*' most dictionaries mention the meanings 'house', 'dwelling', 'temple', 'household', 'nation' etc., but not 'world'. This philological incorrectness might stem from a well-used Indonesian reference, but it is of minor influence for the following argumentation.

[56] *Kamus Besar Bahasa Indonesia* (*Comprehensive Dictionary of the Indonesian Language*), 3rd edition, page 287.

[57] *Kamus Besar Bahasa Indonesia*, 3rd edition, page 157.

business is its aim. Economy is aimed to manage something in order to bring about life and welfare. Whereas business is aimed to seek maximal profit.

Question 49: Does the Bible also talk about economy and business?

The term 'economy' can be found in the Greek Bible, and is usually translated as stewardship (Indon. *'penatalayanan'*),[58] indicating all kinds of things connected with the management of household affairs.[a]

> a. **1 Kings 4:5-7:** Azariah the son of Nathan, over the officers; Zabud the son of Nathan, a priest *and* the king's friend; Ahishar, over the household; and Adoniram the son of Abda, over the labor force. And Solomon had twelve governors over all Israel, who provided food for the king and his household; each one made provision for one month of the year. (*New King James Version*). – **Numbers 12:7-8:** Not so with my servant Moses; he is entrusted with all my house. With him I speak face to face – clearly, not in riddles; and he beholds the form of the LORD. Why then were you not afraid to speak against my servant Moses?

Besides that, different aspects of economy and business are also mentioned in the Bible, such as commandments that regulate the purchase and sale of

---

[58] *Translators' note:* The Indonesian term *'penatalayanan'* ('stewardship') used here has become very popular in church and theology since about the 1970s. The term 'stewardship' was adopted from the theological discussion in the Anglo-Saxon world (also from Dutch theology the term *'rentmeesterschap'* with the same meaning), as a translation of the Greek term *'oikonomia'*. To translate the term 'stewardship' into Indonesian, completely new Indonesian words were created, i.e. *'menatalayani'* ('to steward'), *'penatalayan'* ('steward') and *'penatalayanan'* ('stewardship'), based on the Indonesian verbs *'menata'* ('to order', 'to manage') and *'melayani'* ('to minister', 'to serve'). But until today these newly created words can rarely be found in common Indonesian dictionaries. As scripture references are usually Luke 12:42; 1 Cor. 4:1-2; 1 Peter 4:10 and Titus 1:7 mentioned, where the Greek term *'oikonomos'* can be found in the original Greek text, translated as 'steward' in most English translations. The Greek term *'oikonomia'* is used in the Greek original text of Luke 16:2-4; 1 Cor. 9:17; Eph. 3:2; Col. 1:25 et al., usually rendered as 'stewardship' in many English translations. But ironically in none of these verses the terms *'oikonomos'* or *'oikonomia'* are translated as *'penatalayan(an)'* in the Indonesian Bible translations (except the so-called *Indonesian Literal Translation* propagated by the Yahweh-Movement). Whereas the Catechism-Update itself cites 1 Kings 4:6, where the Greek term *'oikonomos'* is found in its Greek (Septuagint) translation of the Hebrew word *'al-beyt* ('over the house'), rendered as 'over the household' in the *KJV* and other English translations. The Greek (Septuagint) translation of Num. 12:7 does not use the term *'oikonomos'*, but the meaning of the term is paraphrased as "*en holo oikos mou pistos estin*", as an equivalent of the Hebrew "*bekol beyti ne'eman hu*'", which is rendered as "he is entrusted with all my house" in the *New Revised Standard Version*.

D. Realm of Economy

goods, concerning agriculture and animal husbandry, also the dealings toward the poor,[b] children, orphans, widows[c] and the environment.[d]

    b. **Exodus 23:6**: You shall not pervert the justice due to your poor in their lawsuits.
    – **Deuteronomy 15:7-11**: If there is among you anyone in need, a member of your community in any of your towns within the land that the LORD your God is giving you, do not be hard-hearted or tight-fisted toward your needy neighbor. You should rather open your hand, willingly lending enough to meet the need, whatever it may be. Be careful that you do not entertain a mean thought, thinking, "The seventh year, the year of remission, is near", and therefore view your needy neighbor with hostility and give nothing; your neighbor might cry to the LORD against you, and you would incur guilt. Give liberally and be ungrudging when you do so, for on this account the LORD your God will bless you in all your work and in all that you undertake. Since there will never cease to be some in need on the earth, I therefore command you, "Open your hand to the poor and needy neighbor in your land."

    c. **Deuteronomy 24:19-22**: When you reap your harvest in your field and forget a sheaf in the field, you shall not go back to get it; it shall be left for the alien, the orphan, and the widow, so that the LORD your God may bless you in all your undertakings. When you beat your olive trees, do not strip what is left; it shall be for the alien, the orphan, and the widow. When you gather the grapes of your vineyard, do not glean what is left; it shall be for the alien, the orphan, and the widow. Remember that you were a slave in the land of Egypt; therefore I am commanding you to do this.

    d. **Leviticus 25:21-24**: I will order my blessing for you in the sixth year, so that it will yield a crop for three years. When you sow in the eighth year, you will be eating from the old crop; until the ninth year, when its produce comes in, you shall eat the old. The land shall not be sold in perpetuity, for the land is mine; with me you are but aliens and tenants. Throughout the land that you hold, you shall provide for the redemption of the land.

Also the ordinances concerning the Year of Jubilee are very much connected to economy, as they are meant to overcome economic difficulties in a situation of slavery and poverty.[e]

    e. **Leviticus 25:8-25.**

Issues of economy and business can also be found in the New Testament, e.g. Jesus' Parable of the Talents.[f]

    f. **Matthew 25:14-30.**

Question 50: The Bible indeed talks a lot about economy and business. So what then is the biblical view of economy and business enterprises?

Basically the Bible regards economy and business as honorable enterprises. Why is that so?

Firstly, God is the Creator of everything in this world. Everything has been created in a very good condition.[a] So everything in this world, including economy and business, is a part of God's good creation.

> a. **Genesis 1:31a**: God saw everything that he had made, and indeed, it was very good.

Secondly, God created humans as extraordinary creatures, i.e. images of God.[b] In this condition humans become God's mandatories on the earth, bearing the mandate to manage and order the earth and all that is in it. Thus man is called to become an '*oikonomos*' ('economist') on the earth. Man is called to make the earth a comfortable and beautiful place to live on, capable to supply the necessities of human life. Finally by economic enterprises humans can bring about a good life and thereby glorify God.

> b. **Genesis 1:27**: So God created humankind in his image, in the image of God he created them; male and female he created them. (Comp. *Heidelberg Catechism*, question no. 6).

Based on these two principles, engagement in economy and business means to carry out the mandate of God, i.e. to manage and order God's creation on the earth responsibly. So it can be concluded that economy and business are honorable enterprises because they are a tangible form of obedience towards God's commandments in order to bring about a good life in this world.

Question 51: Basically economy and business are firmly rooted in the mandate of God. Why then do many Christians think that economy and business are dirty endeavors?

The opinion that economy and business are dirty endeavors is caused by two facts: *Firstly* there is a view that material things are of minor value. All material things are bad, evil and sinful, hinder humans from encountering God and entering heaven.[a]

> a. **Matthew 6:19-24**: "Do not store up for yourselves treasures on earth, where moth and rust consume and where thieves break in and steal; but store up for yourselves treasures in heaven, where neither moth nor rust consumes and where thieves do not break in and steal. For where your treasure is, there your heart will be also."
> "The eye is the lamp of the body. So, if your eye is healthy, your whole body will

D. Realm of Economy

be full of light; but if your eye is unhealthy, your whole body will be full of darkness. If then the light in you is darkness, how great is the darkness!" "No one can serve two masters; for a slave will either hate the one and love the other, or be devoted to the one and despise the other. You cannot serve God and wealth." – **1 Timothy 6:10**: For the love of money is a root of all kinds of evil. Some people, eager for money, have wandered from the faith and pierced themselves with many griefs. (*New International Version*).

The *second* reason stems from the realm of economy and business itself, exactly speaking from humans who execute economy and business. Often they run their enterprises by justifying all kinds of methods, they are greedy, deceitful, mendacious and they give bribes.[b] Such behavior causes of economy and business to have a dirty image.

    b. **Amos 8:4-6**: Hear this, you that trample on the needy, and bring to ruin the poor of the land, saying, "When will the new moon be over so that we may sell grain; and the sabbath, so that we may offer wheat for sale? We will make the ephah small and the shekel great, and practice deceit with false balances, buying the poor for silver and the needy for a pair of sandals, and selling the sweepings of the wheat." (Comp. *Heidelberg Catechism*, question no. 110).

Question 52: How then do Christians run economy and business?

When active in economy and business Christians always have to remember that God is the Creator of all things.[a] This implies the confession that God is the Source, Lord and only Owner of everything.[b]

    a. **Genesis 1:1-31**. (Comp. *Heidelberg Catechism*, question no. 1).

    b. **1 Corinthians 10:26**: for "the earth and its fullness are the Lord's." (Comp. Psalm 24:1).

Therefore nothing is out of the power of God, including economy and business matters. God has created everything according to His plan that is to bring about the well-being of the whole creation.

Starting from that confession, every Christian engaged in economy and business should direct his whole attitude and behavior according to that plan of God, in order to create a state of well-being for the whole creation to glorify God. Christians are not allowed to run economy and business just for themselves, to gain profit or to attain financial success. To strive for profit, to accumulate capital or even financial success are indeed not forbidden. Nevertheless, they should not become an end in itself. All this is just a means or tool to achieve the final and more honorable goal, i.e. to bring about the well-being of the whole creation in order to glorify God.[c]

    c. **1 Corinthians 10:31**: So, whether you eat or drink, or whatever you do, do everything for the glory of God. – Proverbs 3:9: Honor the LORD with your wealth, With the best of all your income, (*New Jewish Publishing Society Tanakh*). (Comp. *Heidelberg Catechism*, question no. 111).

Question 53: How can we accomplish the plan of God in the aforementioned realm of economy and business?

Mankind has been given the right to manage and utilize creation only for the sake of facilitating life together. Therefore it is unrighteous if the creation is used only for one's own interests.[a] Aware of the fact, that everything belongs to God, Christians are also obliged to give back to God a reasonable sum[59] of their proceeds of economy and business.[b]

> a. **Romans 11:36**: For from him and through him and to him are all things. To him be the glory forever. ...
>
> b. **Deuteronomy 16:16b-17**: They shall not appear before the LORD empty-handed; all shall give as they are able, according to the blessing of the LORD your God that he has given you.

Besides that Christians have to be ready to share a part of these proceeds with their neighbors in need as an expression of solidarity without making any distinctions.[c]

> c. **Galatians 6:2**: Bear one another's burdens, and in this way you will fulfill the law of Christ.

It has to be kept in mind that all outcomes of economy and business which are shared with God and the neighbors are not charities or alms, but an obligation and an honor due to God. On this basis Christians are also obliged to defend the rights of the poor in order to bring about a socially balanced living

---

[59] *Translators' note:* In some congregations of the GKJTU the members are summoned to give the tithe but in other congregations of the GKJTU 10% are regarded as too legalistic, even more because Pentecostal churches collect the tithe from their members by all possible means. Therefore the Catechism-Update only uses the term 'a reasonable sum' and cites Deut. 16:16-17 (not Mal. 3:10 etc.). This contribution for the local congregation is understood as an offering for God. Whereas contributions for social or diaconal purposes are distinguished from those offerings. As many Asians are generous only towards the members of their extended family, it has to be stressed that these offerings must be given 'without making any distinctions'. Theologically it is being stressed, that those contributions should not be regarded as charities and alms, they are not given at will, but are "an obligation and an honor due to God", the Lord to whom everything belongs. Therefore the Catechism-Update stresses again and again that Christians only give back to God what is already His. Thus the term 'reasonable sum' gets its full meaning.

D. Realm of Economy

together. It must not happen that the rich become always richer and the poorer always poorer.[d]

    d. **Matthew 25:35-36**: ... for I was hungry and you gave me food, I was thirsty and you gave me something to drink, I was a stranger and you welcomed me, I was naked and you gave me clothing, I was sick and you took care of me, I was in prison and you visited me.

Question 54: Is the church as an institution allowed to engage in economic and business activities?

Yes, she is allowed to, as long as these activities are for the welfare of the church members and of society,[a] support the threefold calling of the Church for fellowship,[b] witness[c] and service,[d] or promote the financial self-support of the church.[e]

    a. **Jeremiah 29:7**: But seek the welfare of the city where I have sent you into exile, and pray to the LORD on its behalf, for in its welfare you will find your welfare.

    b. **Hebrews 10:25**: We should not stay away from our assembly, as is the custom of some, but encourage one another, and this all the more as you see the day drawing near. (*New American Bible*).

    c. **Matthew 28:19-20**: Go therefore and make disciples of all nations, baptizing them in the name of the Father and of the Son and of the Holy Spirit, and teaching them to obey everything that I have commanded you. And remember, I am with you always, to the end of the age.

    d. **Romans 12:11**: Do not lag in zeal, be ardent in spirit, serve the Lord.

    e. See Master Plan for the Development of the GKJTU for the years 2003-2028, especially chapter V, point B.2c.[60]

---

[60] *Translators' note:* In the original version of the Catechism-Update reference is made to the 25-Year-Master-Plan of the GKJTU, without explicitly citing it. But as there is until now no complete, official translation of that Master Plan, we hereby present a translation of the passage referred to: "Financial self-support does not just mean the ability to finance oneself. In its wholeness self-support comprehends all efforts of the church to raise, manage, multiply, safeguard and to use the available funds in a responsible way to carry out the mission of the Church. Therefore self-support neither means to receive nor to give any funds to or from other bodies. In the spirit of self-support the church has to be able to manage all available funds, either from inside or from outside, in a serious and responsible way. Financial self-support is closely related to independence in the field of theology and human resources. A sound theological understanding, supported by adequately qualified human resources will contribute significantly towards financial self-support. Since its 26th General Synod Assembly [2003] the GKJTU realizes the need for financial self-support. In the future the GKJTU will no longer be able to be completely dependent

Question 55: If the church is thus allowed to engage in economic and business activities, in what kind of activities may the church be engaged?

The church is allowed to engage in all kind of enterprises which are not contrary to Christian faith, the Church Order and Bylaws of the GKJTU, and which are ordered by special regulations.[61]

---

on the support of its domestic and overseas partners. The GKJTU has already begun to prepare itself by starting projects for financial self-support. In the future these projects will have to be developed further."

[61] ***Translators' note:*** It would by far exceed the scope of this Update to clarify all aspects of church law, civil law and common law concerning Christian fund raising foundations. Therefore this answer is restricted to the general instruction that these enterprises must not be contrary to Christian faith and ethics in general and the Church Order and Bylaw of the GKJTU in particular. Unfortunately the 'special regulations' mentioned here have not yet been issued.

E. Realm of Science and Technology

Question 56: What is the meaning of science and technology?[62]

Science is the rational, logical and systematic interlink age of different human insights concerning God and His creation in order to glorify the Creator. Whereas technology refers to the outcomes of the practical application of scientific knowledge, which comprises the whole process of planning, designing, assembling, testing and maintenance of a whole system or a specific product, e.g. sickles, biogas technology, crossbreeding, sewing machines, computers etc. Progress in technology is influenced by the results of scientific research. On the other hand, science uses technology to gain progress.

Science and technology are products of human reason which is a gracious gift of God in order that mankind can responsibly manage His creation[a] and finally glorify the name of the Lord.[b]

    a. **Genesis 1:28**: God blessed them, and God said to them, "Be fruitful and multiply, and fill the earth and subdue it; and have dominion over the fish of the sea and over the birds of the air and over every living thing that moves upon the earth." (Comp. also **Genesis 2:15**, cited below with question no. 56 as citation c.).

    b. **Colossians 3:17**: And whatever you do, in word or deed, do everything in the name of the Lord Jesus, giving thanks to God the Father through him. – **Matthew 22:37**: He said to him, 'You shall love the Lord your God with all your heart, and with all your soul, and with all your mind.' (Comp. also **Psalm 8:2,4-7,10**, cited below with question no. 57 as citation b.).

---

[62] *Translators' note:* For the Indonesian term '*ilmu pengetahuan dan teknik*' / '*teknologi*' ("science, humanities and technology") the Indonesian language often uses the abbreviation or acronym '*iptek*'. During the various revisions of the Catechism-Update it was decided to replace the acronym '*iptek*' by the extent term '*ilmu pengetahuan dan teknologi*', which makes the wording sometimes a little bit clumsy, both in the Indonesian original text and in the translations. Even more in English, where the term 'science' actually is restricted to the 'exact sciences' only, and there is strictly speaking no general English term comprising both 'exact sciences' and 'humanities', which are sometimes even called 'arts'. Thus the Indonesian term '*iptek*' often has to be put into English as 'science, humanities and technology' or 'science, arts and technology'.

Question 57: Why do humans possess science, humanities and technology?

In His great love, the Lord created humankind according to the image and likeness of God.[a]

   a. **Genesis 1:26**: Then God said, "Let us make humankind in our image, according to our likeness; and let them have dominion over the fish of the sea, and over the birds of the air, and over the cattle, and over all the wild animals of the earth, and over every creeping thing that creeps upon the earth." (Comp. *Heidelberg Catechism*, question no. 6).

Then God granted a part of His sovereignty unto humankind to investigate nature,[b] so that humans might adore the work of God, also have dominion over, cultivate and keep the whole creation of God.[c]

   b. **Psalm 8:1,3-6,9**: O LORD, our Sovereign, how majestic is your name in all the earth! You have set your glory above the heavens. .... When I look at your heavens, the work of your fingers, the moon and the stars that you have established; what are human beings that you are mindful of them, mortals that you care for them? Yet you have made them a little lower than God, and crowned them with glory and honor. You have given them dominion over the works of your hands; you have put all things under their feet, ... O LORD, our Sovereign, how majestic is your name in all the earth!

   c. **Genesis 2:15**: The LORD God took the man and put him in the garden of Eden to till it and keep it.

In order that humans can carry out that mandate, God gave human reason, so that humans can design and construct science, humanities, technology and also fine arts.[d]

   d. **Genesis 4:19-22b**: Lamech took two wives; the name of the one was Adah, and the name of the other Zillah. Adah bore Jabal; he was the ancestor of those who live in tents and have livestock. His brother's name was Jubal; he was the ancestor of all those who play the lyre and pipe. Zillah bore Tubal-cain, who made all kinds of bronze and iron tools.

Thus science, arts and technology are gracious gifts of God, which are one of the distinctives that make humans differ from other creatures.[e]

   e. **Job 35:11**: God ... Who gives us more knowledge than the beasts of the earth, makes us wiser than the birds of the sky ... (*New Jewish Publishing Society Tanakh*).

E. Realm of Science and Technology

Question 58: Are science and technology not contrary to human destiny ('*kodrat*')?

In general '*kodrat*'[63] is understood as the absolute omnipotence of God who decrees the fate of every human. In other words, human life is inevitably decreed by the power of God. This concept is not in accordance with Christian faith. Humans need not accept the conditions of nature as inevitable destiny ('*kodrat*').[a]

 a. **Genesis 30:35-39**: But that day Laban removed the male goats that were striped and spotted, and all the female goats that were speckled and spotted, every one that had white on it, and every lamb that was black, and put them in charge of his sons; …. Then Jacob took fresh rods of poplar and almond and plane, and peeled white streaks in them, exposing the white of the rods. He set the rods that he had peeled in front of the flocks in the troughs, that is, the watering places, where the flocks came to drink. And since they bred when they came to drink, the flocks bred in front of the rods, and so the flocks produced young that were striped, speckled, and spotted.

Humans have to manage and order nature in freedom and responsibility, based on their God-given sovereignty. Notwithstanding the fact that God created this world as 'very good',[b] He deliberately gave mankind the mandate to manage and further develop His creation.[c]

 b. **Genesis 1:31**: God saw everything that he had made, and indeed, it was very good. And there was evening and there was morning, the sixth day.

 c. **Genesis 1:26-28; 5:1-3**, extent quotations with question no. 59 below, quotation a.

---

[63] *Translators' note:* The Arabic loan word '*kodrat*' in the Indonesian language (from Arabic قدر – *qadar*) denotes one of the six articles (*Aquidah*) of Sunni-Islam. It denotes first the supreme power of God, than specifically the things decreed by God's supreme power or at least foreknown by God: the laws of nature, the predispositions and the destiny of every individual. Islamic theologians and also folk Islam differ about the issue how far the individual destiny of every human is predestined by God and whether technological efforts are contrary to divine destiny. But in general God's supreme power, omniscience and predestination are very much stressed in Islam. Within Christian theology (and also within other religions) there were and there are also different views concerning the issue of divine predestination decreeing the temporal fate and eternal salvation of humans, also concerning the issue whether humans do or do not transgress their God-given limits by certain achievements of technology. In the context of a Muslim majority stressing God's supreme power and predestination, many Indonesian churches are quite reluctant to accept the Christian doctrine of divine predestination as taught by both Martin Luther and John Calvin.

Thus the omnipotence of God is visible not only in God-created nature, but also in the creativity of humans.

Thus science and technology are not contrary to human destiny ('*kodrat*'). Science and technology just develop, build up and improve human life if applied in responsibility.

Question 59: Does that mean that God has completely surrendered His creation into the hands of mankind?

God has indeed given sovereignty to humans to have dominion over, cultivate and keep the whole creation of God. But God does still guide humans by His Word when applying science and technology in order to manage Creation.[a]

> a. **Genesis 1:27-28**: So God created humankind in his image, in the image of God he created them; male and female he created them. God blessed them, and God said to them, "Be fruitful and multiply, and fill the earth and subdue it; and have dominion over the fish of the sea and over the birds of the air and over every living thing that moves upon the earth." – **Genesis 2:16-17**: And the LORD God commanded the man, "You may freely eat of every tree of the garden; but of the tree of the knowledge of good and evil you shall not eat, for in the day that you eat of it you shall die." – **Genesis 5:1b**: When God created humankind, he made them in the likeness of God. – **Deuteronomy 11:26-28**: See, I am setting before you today a blessing and a curse: the blessing, if you obey the commandments of the LORD your God that I am commanding you today; and the curse, if you do not obey the commandments of the LORD your God, but turn from the way that I am commanding you today, to follow other gods that you have not known.

By His Spirit God is involved in every technological achievement of mankind in order to keep and develop His creation.[b]

> b. **Exodus 31:2-4:** See, I have called by name Bezalel the son of Uri, son of Hur, of the tribe of Judah: and I have filled him with the Spirit of God, with ability and intelligence, with knowledge and all craftsmanship, to devise artistic designs, to work in gold, silver, and bronze … (*Revised Standard Version* – comp. also **Exodus 28:3; 35:31**) – **Romans 8:28**: We know that in everything God works for good with those who love him, who are called according to his purpose. (*Revised Standard Version*).

But as humans were created as limited creatures, therefore all achievements of human science and technology are of limited value, too.[c]

> c. **Isaiah 40:6b:** All mankind is grass, and all their glory like the flower of the field (*New American Bible*).

E. Realm of Science and Technology

The achievements of human technology are great yet never perfect. Its benefits are still dependent on the blessing of God and open to His plans.[d]

- d. **Proverbs 16:9**: A man's heart deviseth his way: but the LORD directeth his steps. (*King James Version* – comp. also **Job 31:4; 34:21**). (Comp. *Heidelberg Catechism*, question no. 1, also question 27-28).

Question 60: Why can science and technology also be used to damage God's creation?

After the Fall human reason is darkened[a] and inclined to evil.[b]

- a. **Ephesians 4:17-18**: This I say therefore, and testify in the Lord, that ye henceforth walk not as other Gentiles walk, in the vanity of their mind, Having the understanding darkened, being alienated from the life of God through the ignorance that is in them, because of the blindness of their heart. (*King James Version*).
- b. **Genesis 6:5**: The LORD saw that the wickedness of humankind was great in the earth, and that every inclination of the thoughts of their hearts was only evil continually. – **Mark 7:20-21**: And he said, 'It is what comes out of a person that defiles. For it is from within, from the human heart, that evil intentions come: fornication, theft, murder.' (Comp. *Heidelberg Catechism*, question no. 7 and no. 13).

Even human works with the best intentions often have fatal results.[c]

- c. **Romans 7:19**: For I do not do the good I want, but the evil I do not want is what I do. – **Proverbs 14:12**: There is a way that seems right to a person, but its end is the way to death.

Therefore all results of scientific research and technological achievements in the fields of social sciences, theology, physics, engineering, information technology etc. will never reach unto the very essence of truth. Humans are even inclined to misuse science and technology to rival God,[d] to idolize[e] science and technology itself,[f] so that they fancy they did not need to rely on God any more.[g]

- d. **Genesis 11:4**: Then they said, "Come, let us build ourselves a city, and a tower with its top in the heavens, and let us make a name for ourselves; otherwise we shall be scattered abroad upon the face of the whole earth."
- e. **Isaiah 44:9-13**: All who make idols are nothing, and the things they delight in do not profit; their witnesses neither see nor know. And so they will be put to shame. Who would fashion a god or cast an image that can do no good? Look, all its devotees shall be put to shame; the artisans too are merely human. Let them all assemble, let them stand up; they shall be terrified, they shall all be put to shame. The ironsmith fashions it and works it over the coals, shaping it with hammers, and forging it with his strong arm; he becomes hungry and his strength fails, he drinks no water and is faint. The carpenter stretches a line,

marks it out with a stylus, fashions it with planes, and marks it with a compass; he makes it in human form, with human beauty, to be set up in a shrine

f. **Colossians 2:8:** See to it that no one takes you captive by philosophy and empty deceit, according to human tradition, according to the elemental spirits of the world, and not according to Christ. (*English Standard Version*).

g. **Psalm 10:4-6**: In the pride of their countenance the wicked say, "God will not seek it out"; all their thoughts are, "There is no God." Their ways prosper at all times; your judgments are on high, out of their sight; as for their foes, they scoff at them. They think in their heart, "We shall not be moved; throughout all generations we shall not meet adversity."

Science and technology are also often used to kill fellow-humans and destroy the whole creation of God.[h]

h. **Hosea 4:1-3**: Hear the word of the LORD, O people of Israel; for the LORD has an indictment against the inhabitants of the land. There is no faithfulness or loyalty, and no knowledge of God in the land. Swearing, lying, and murder, and stealing and adultery break out; bloodshed follows bloodshed. Therefore the land mourns, and all who live in it languish; together with the wild animals and the birds of the air, even the fish of the sea are perishing

Thus all works of men are corrupted by sin and therefore can bring about both blessing and disaster.[64] Even the best achievements of science and technology inevitably bring about negative side effects, too. The scientific and technological efforts to overcome these negative side effects can still bring about new negative side effects.

Question 61: Thus science and technology can become both a blessing and a curse. Which examples can be cited for this?

As the simplest example, a sickle can be used to earn ones livelihood, but also to kill one's fellow-men. In the modern world television, videos, newspapers, periodicals and other media can be used to spread the Gospel, useful

---

[64] *Translators' note:* The paradoxical nature of science and technology is one of the basic thoughts in questions and answers no. 60-69: On the one hand many achievements of science and technology can be received with thanksgiving as a blessing from God. On the other hand almost all technical achievements have at least some negative side-effects. This paradoxical idea rejects both a blind technophobia as well as a too optimistic view concerning technical progress. In the first drafts of the Catechism-Update the Indonesian term '*laknat*' ('curse') was consequently used as the contrary of '*berkat*' ('blessing', 'benefit'), but during its revisions '*laknat*' was replaced by '*bencana*' ('disaster', 'accident', 'calamity'). In the English translation 'curse', 'disaster', 'disastrous aspects', 'negative effects' etc. are used alternately as terms contrary to 'blessing'.

E. Realm of Science and Technology

information, valuable entertainment etc. But these media can also be misused to spread pornography, lies or even atheism. Even the best media still can make people lethargic[a] and nurture an attitude of consumerism.

> a. **Proverbs 6:9-10**: How long will you lie there, O lazybones? When will you rise from your sleep? A little sleep, a little slumber, a little folding of the hands to rest ...

Also means of transportation such as motorbikes, cars, airplanes etc. can be used for good and for bad purposes. But even the best means of transportation causes pollution, uses up fuel and always brings about the risk of accidents.[b]

> b. **Isaiah 24:5-6**: The earth lies polluted under its inhabitants; for they have transgressed laws, violated the statutes, broken the everlasting covenant. Therefore a curse devours the earth, and its inhabitants suffer for their guilt; therefore the inhabitants of the earth dwindled, and few people are left.

As yet another example, the academic discipline of history can be used to adore God's work within human history and draw lessons from past events. But if used unwisely, historical sciences can also be used to launch attacks against biblical truths.

Question 62: One very obvious and perceptible negative effect of science and technology is the destruction of the environment. How do science and technology destroy the environment?

Firstly, science and technology need natural resources for their further development. Mining and using these natural resources very often damages the ecosystem, the biological balance of the environment. If this natural balance is disturbed, that disturbance has various effects for future life, such as new diseases appearing, pests getting out of control etc. This damage to the natural system might happen as an inevitable side effect of the use of science and technology. But it can also be a result of an exorbitant mining and use of natural resources in order to develop science and technology.[a]

> a. **Numbers 11:4a**: The rabble who were among them had greedy desires; ... (*New American Standard Bible*). – **Luke 12:15**: And he said to them, 'Take care! Be on your guard against all kinds of greed; for one's life does not consist in the abundance of possessions.'

Secondly, the use of scientific and technological products very often destroys the environment, too. In this case also the destruction of the environment might be an inevitable side effect of the use of scientific and technological products, or it might be a result of misuse of science and technology, or the destruction of the environment might even be the ultimate aim of certain technologies and scientific research. To illustrate the destruction of the environment as a side effect when scientific and technological products are used, one example are motor vehicles which emit fumes which pollute the air and worsen the greenhouse effect; another example in this realm is the use of propellants (aerosol) and coolants (freon), which damage the ozone layer of the earth. For the misuse of science and technology which destroys the environment, electro fishing and cyanide fishing can be mentioned as examples,[65] as these methods kill all fish around.[b] The environment is deliberately destroyed by e.g. the nuclear bomb which utterly destroys a whole area.

> b. **Hosea 4:1-3**: Hear the word of the LORD, O people of Israel; for the LORD has an indictment against the inhabitants of the land. There is no faithfulness or loyalty, and no knowledge of God in the land. Swearing, lying, and murder, and stealing and adultery break out; bloodshed follows bloodshed. Therefore the land mourns, and all who live in it languish; together with the wild animals and the birds of the air, even the fish of the sea are perishing.

Thirdly, science and technology produce tools and machines by which natural resources can be more and more easily exploited. Together with boundless human greed and wishes, this easiness of application results in big scale mining of natural resources without taking the ecological balance into account. As an example, the invention of the motor saw made it much easier to fell huge trees and to log vast areas.[c] These vast deforestations contribute to global warming and world-wide climate changes, landslides, floods everywhere and shortages of drinking water.[d]

> c. **Isaiah 37:24**: Through your servants you have blasphemed my Lord. Because you thought, 'Thanks to my vast chariotry, It is I who have climbed the highest mountains, To the remotest parts of the Lebanon, And have cut down its loftiest cedars, Its choicest cypresses, And have reached its highest peak, Its densest forest. (*New Jewish Publishing Society Tanakh*). (Comp. also Deuteronomy 20:19).
>
> d. **Jeremiah 4:22a, 23, 25-26a**: For my people are foolish, they do not know me; … I looked on the earth, and lo, it was waste and void; and to the heavens, and

---

[65] *Translators' note:* Blast fishing, electro fishing and cyanide fishing are actually forbidden in Indonesia. But for various reason the authorities do not take stern actions against the offenders, as these seem not to have another source of income. Thus many coral reefs and fish stocks have already been destroyed. The only effective means against it are the efforts of environmentalist groups who make the fishermen and the village chiefs conscious that these methods in the long run destroy the livelihood of the fishermen themselves.

E. Realm of Science and Technology

they had no light. ... I looked, and lo, there was no one at all, and all the birds of the air had fled. I looked, and lo, the fruitful land was a desert.

Fourthly, the products of science and technology which are no longer used finally become waste, which pollutes and destroys our environment.[e] As an example, plastics, tins and many other human products which are no longer used become hazardous waste which threatens all forms of life.

   e. **Ephesians 4:19**: they have become callous and have given themselves up to licentiousness, greedy to practice every kind of uncleanness. (*Revised Standard Version*). – **Ephesians 5:3.5**: But fornication, and all uncleanness, or covetousness, let it not be once named among you, as becometh saints ... For this ye know, that no whoremonger, nor unclean person, nor covetous man, who is an idolater, hath any inheritance in the kingdom of Christ and of God. (*King James Version*).

Question 63: What are the effects of this destruction of the environment for human life and for life in general?

The earth or the whole environment is the place and also the source of all life, including human life. Thus the destruction of the environment threatens all forms of life, including human life. One example is global warming. Global warming leads to irregular climate change, life destroying storms and floods, all kinds of diseases which humans cannot resist, deglaciation of the polar caps which in turn makes the sea level rise and threatens life at the coast lines.[a]

   a. **Jeremiah 12:10.13**: Many shepherds have destroyed my vineyard, they have trampled down my portion, they have made my pleasant portion a desolate wilderness. ... They have sown wheat and have reaped thorns, they have tired themselves out but profit nothing. They shall be ashamed of their harvests because of the fierce anger of the LORD. – **Ezekiel 26:19-20**: For thus says the Lord GOD: When I make you a city laid waste, like cities that are not inhabited, when I bring up the deep over you, and the great waters cover you, then I will thrust you down ..., so that you will not be inhabited or have a place in the land of the living.

Question 64: The sin of man influences science and technology in a special form in Indonesia. What is that special form?

For many reasons science and technology create new dependencies and a growing gap between the industrial nations and the developing nations. The industrial nations have an increasing command of science and technology, whereas most developing nations just consume the products of science and technology produced by the industrial nations. This fact makes the developing nations more and more dependent on foreign technology.[a]

> a. **1 Samuel 13:19-20**: Now there was no smith to be found throughout all the land of Israel; for the Philistines said, 'The Hebrews must not make swords or spears for themselves'; so all the Israelites went down to the Philistines to sharpen their plowshare, mattocks, axes, or sickles; ...

To be able to afford this foreign technology the developing nations have to sell their natural resources (such as oil, gas, wood, gold etc.) at a relatively low price. The gains of these sales are further reduced by the high costs of mining and logging by foreign companies and corruption. This structure also results in big social gaps within the developing nations themselves. Some of the above-mentioned products of technology are only affordable for a small segment of society from the middle class upward. Whereas the vast poor majority of the society become victims of the negative side effects of science and technology and rather than really being able to enjoy its benefits.[b]

> b. **Amos 6:3.4.6:** O you that put far away the evil day, and bring near a reign of violence? Alas for those who lie on beds of ivory, and lounge on their couches, and eat lambs from the flock, and calves from the stall; ... who drink wine from bowls, and anoint themselves with the finest oils, but are not grieved over the ruin of Joseph!

In the effort to sell their natural resources in order to receive the benefits of science and technology, the people in the developing countries are not aware of their negative effects on nature. Thus, also the Indonesian nation sells its abundant natural riches for the short pleasures offered by technological progress.[c]

> c. **Genesis 25:30-34**: Esau said to Jacob, 'Let me eat some of that red stuff, for I am famished!' ... Jacob said, 'First sell me your birthright.' Esau said, 'I am about to die; of what use is a birthright to me?' Jacob said, 'Swear to me first.' So he swore to him, and sold his birthright to Jacob. Then Jacob gave Esau bread and lentil stew, and he ate and drank, and rose and went his way. Thus Esau despised his birthright.

Question 65: Can science, humanities and technology help mankind to return to God?

Answer: After falling into sin humans find it difficult to understand God in the way they could before the Fall.[a]

> a. **Job 37:23**: The Almighty – we cannot *fathom* him; he is great in power and justice, and abundant righteousness he will not violate. (*New Revised Standard Version, modified based on the official Indonesian Translation*). – **Psalm 82:5**:

E. Realm of Science and Technology

They have neither knowledge nor understanding, they walk around in darkness; all the foundations of the earth are shaken.

So humans make strong efforts to know God[b] again through His creation,[c] by using their reason. Through natural science, technology, sociology and also theology humans can again know about God and His power.[d]

- b. **Acts 17:27-28**: ... so that they would search for God and perhaps grope for him and find him – though indeed he is not far from each one of us. For 'In him we live and move and have our being'; as even some of your own poets have said, 'For we too are his offspring.' (Comp. *GKJTU-Update of the Heidelberg Catechism*, question no. 20-21 above).

- c. **Job 12:7-10**: "But ask the animals, and they will teach you; the birds of the air, and they will tell you; ask the plants of the earth, and they will teach you; and the fish of the sea will declare to you. Who among all these does not know that the hand of the LORD has done this? In his hand is the life of every living thing and the breath of every human being."

- d. **Romans 1:19-20**: For what can be known about God is plain to them, because God has shown it to them. Ever since the creation of the world his eternal power and divine nature, invisible though they are, have been understood and seen through the things he has made. So they are without excuse; ...

But to get back to God in a state as before the Fall, humans have to believe in God and worship Him through His Word which has become man in Jesus Christ.[e]

- e. **John 1:14**: And the Word became flesh and lived among us, and we have seen his glory, the glory as of a father's only son, full of grace and truth. (Comp. *Heidelberg Catechism*, question no. 19).

Question 66: Does salvation in Christ also affect science, humanities and technology?

In Christ God[66] has atoned for the sins of mankind and renewed the human mind.[a]

- a. **Romans 12:2**: Do not be conformed to this world, but be transformed by the renewing of your minds, so that you may discern what is the will of God – what

---

[66] *Translators' note:* Especially facing the Islamic criticism against the Christian understanding of trinity, the formula "God in Christ" (comp. 2 Cor. 5:19) is very important for an Indonesian understanding of the Holy Trinity. Therefore the formula can also be found in the common creed of the Communion of Churches in Indonesia from 1984, paragraph 17 et. al. By this Biblical formula it is made clear, that Jesus Christ is not a second deity besides God the Father – even if not all Trinitarian Questions can be answered by this biblical formula.

is good and acceptable and perfect. (Comp. *Heidelberg Catechism*, question no. 45 and question no. 86).

Everyone who believes in this atonement of Christ will receive the Holy Spirit[b] to get a new, thankful attitude towards science, humanities and technology.

> b. **Acts 2:38**: Peter said to them, "Repent, and be baptized every one of you in the name of Jesus Christ so that your sins may be forgiven; and you will receive the gift of the Holy Spirit."

With an attitude of fearing God[c] and with the help of the Holy Spirit[d] the believers can get an even clearer knowledge, so that they can make good and responsible use of science, humanities and technology, also to discern between the blessings and the disastrous aspects of science and technology. Thus the disastrous aspects can be minimized and the blessings can be maximized for the glory of God.

> c. **Psalm 111:10**: The fear of the LORD is the beginning of wisdom; all those who practice it have a good understanding. His praise endures forever.
>
> d. **Daniel 5:12a**: … because an excellent spirit, knowledge, and understanding to interpret dreams, explain riddles, and solve problems were found in this Daniel, whom the king named Belteshazzar.

Question 67: How can believers discern between the blessings and the disastrous aspects of science, humanities and technology?

Every believer is called to attain a maximal knowledge about science, humanities and technology, as these are gifts of God. With this knowledge the believers are called to weigh up against each other the positive and the negative effects of every scientific and technological achievement – not only the effects for humans, but also the effects for the whole creation.[a]

> a. **1 Corinthians 10:23**: 'All things are lawful', but not all things are beneficial. 'All things are lawful', but not all things build up. – **1 Corinthians 2:15**: The spiritual man judges all things, but is himself to be judged by no one. (*Revised Standard Version*).

Christians should not fall into a blind scientism and should not let themselves be infected by a technology-and-science-fever. They rather should be able to discern what is pleasing to God and what is not.[b]

> b. **Romans 12:2**: Do not be conformed to this world, but be transformed by the renewing of your minds, so that you may discern what is the will of God – what is good and acceptable and perfect. (Comp. Ephesians 4:23).

E. Realm of Science and Technology

By example, the believer will weigh up the benefit of a motor vehicle against the air pollution and risks of accident it brings about.

In an attitude of fearing God the believers will ponder whether a certain technological achievement is within the God-given borders of mankind or whether it is a form of human arrogance and revolt against God.[c]

   c. **2 Kings 19:23**: Through your envoys you have blasphemed my Lord. Because you thought, 'Thanks to my vast chariotry, It is I who have climbed the highest mountains, To the remotest parts of the Lebanon, And have cut down its loftiest cedars, Its choicest cypresses, And have reached its remotest lodge, Its densest forest.' (*New Jewish Publishing Society Tanakh*).

Finally Christians are called, to make responsible use of science and technology and minimize its disastrous effects, e.g. by energy saving, by watching TV only as far as useful etc.[d] Believers will also fight against the misuse of science and technology by guiding their fellow-citizens and offering better alternatives.[e] This might mean e.g. to make them aware that pornography corrupts the mentality and to offer responsible sex education as a helpful alternative. Nevertheless, Christians should be motivated to master and use science and technology to a maximum extent in order to bring about blessing for the world. Besides this, Christians can use science and technology by media for the proclamation of the Gospel, e.g. by music, radio, internet, with LCD projectors etc. But if all efforts of science and technology fail, Christians must submit themselves to Almighty God.[f]

   d. **2 Timothy 1:7**: for God did not give us a spirit of cowardice, but rather a spirit of power and of love and of self-discipline.

   e. **2 Timothy 2:24-25a**: And the Lord's servant must not be quarrelsome but kindly to everyone, an apt teacher, patient, correcting opponents with gentleness.

   f. **Proverbs 16:9**: A man's heart deviseth his way: but the LORD directeth his steps. (*King James Version*). (Comp. *Heidelberg Catechism*, question no. 1 and questions 26-28).

However great the achievements of science, humanities and technology might be, Christians are always aware that science and technology always have their inherent weaknesses and the potential to fail. Only God is almighty and perfect.

Question 68: What is our attitude, if the results of science and humanities are contrary to the teachings of the Bible?

It is the same God who has revealed the Bible and who has given reason to mankind. Therefore the Bible and the results of science and humanities should not be in conflict with each other.[a] But as every human is inclined to sin, the results of science and humanities can conflict with human understanding of the Bible. So if the believers face such a conflict, it has to be examined: Is the fault on the side of the scientific result or on the side of the human understanding of the Bible?

> a. **2 Corinthians 1:19-20**: For the Son of God, Jesus Christ, whom we proclaimed among you, Silvanus and Timothy and I, was not 'Yes and No'; but in him it is always 'Yes'. For in him every one of God's promises is a 'Yes'. For this reason it is through him that we say the 'Amen', to the glory of God.

By the guidance of the Holy Spirit, Christians will be able to understand the Bible better and better,[b] so that they can review former interpretations of the Bible. For example, at the times of Galileo Galilei (1564-1642) Christians believed that the heliocentric view (the earth orbiting the sun) was contrary to the Bible. Whereas the Bible nowhere teaches that the sun circles the earth. It has also to be kept in mind that the Bible is not a scientific textbook. God revealed His Word in everyday language for everyday understanding, so that it can be easily understood, even if it is not scientifically exact. E.g. modern man until today says 'the sun rises', although according to exact scientific language the sun does not rise but the earth is rotating forward.

> b. **John 16:13**: When the Spirit of truth comes, he will guide you into all the truth; for he will not speak on his own, but will speak whatever he hears, and he will declare to you the things that are to come.

So Christians have to be aware that biblical faith is well based on tangible acts of God in human history, but faith is not based on historical and scientific proofs.

On the other hand, the results of science and humanities have to be seen critically and one has to discern between irrevocable facts and the ideologies by which this facts are interpreted. E.g. fossils found are irrevocable facts. But if those fossils are than interpreted according to Darwinism, this very interpretation is part of an ideology and can no longer be regarded as pure science. It has to be kept in mind, too, that the results of science are constantly reviewed. Some results of science which might today be regarded in contrary to the Bible might tomorrow be outdated.

Question 69: What is the role of the church, when faith is applied in the field of science, humanities and technology?

Within the communion of believers Christian experts in theological and non-theological fields have a special responsibility to apply Christian faith in the field of science, humanities and technology.[a] This is a very important task

E. Realm of Science and Technology

in order that the whole congregation gets clear standards, especially for ethical issues, how to apply technology. The church is responsible to provide trustworthy information and offer life-long education for these questions.

   a. **Romans 15:1**: We who are strong ought to put up with the failings of the weak, and not to please ourselves. (Comp. *Heidelberg Catechism*, question no. 55).

In the field of science, humanities and technology blessing and curse are always mixed up. There is no scientific or technological achievement which is a pure blessing or a pure curse. Therefore Christians have the responsibility to discern and to choose between the blessings and the curses brought about by science, humanities and technology. The reformational churches cannot leave their members alone with this responsibility and these decisions. Although the reformational churches give each of their members the freedom to make responsible ethical decisions, the church has to provide sufficient information and education under the guidance of the Holy Spirit.[b] Thus every member should be able to make good and right decisions.

   b. **2 Corinthians 3:17**: Now the Lord is the Spirit, and where the Spirit of the Lord is, there is freedom.

In the framework of her mission for the whole creation, the Church always has to utter the truth in order that science, humanities and technology will be used as a blessing for the whole creation,[c] by minimizing their negative side effects.

   c. **Mark 16:15**: And He said to them, 'Go into all the world and preach the gospel to every creature.' (*New King James Version*). – **Romans 8:19**: For the creation waits with eager longing for the revealing of the children of God.

Index

Scripture References – Old Testament

Gen 1:1-31	75
Gen 1:4	22
Gen 1:26	80
Gen 1:27	25, 43, 74
Gen 1:27-28	82
Gen 1:28	59, 60, 62, 79
Gen 1:31	81
Gen 1:31a	74
Gen 2:7	42
Gen 2:15	79, 80
Gen 2:16-17	82
Gen 2:18	29
Gen 4:3-7	43
Gen 4:19-22b	80
Gen 4:20	21
Gen 5:1b	82
Gen 6:5	83
Gen 11:1-9	39
Gen 11:4	83
Gen 17:10	31
Gen 25:30-34	88
Gen 30:35-39	81
Ex 23:6	73
Ex 23:25	33
Ex 28:3	82
Ex 31:2-4	82
Lev 19:31	23
Lev 25:8-25	73
Lev 25:21-24	73
Num 11:4a	85
Num 12:7-8	72
Deut 4:19b	44
Deut 7:3-4	51
Deut 11:26-28	82
Deut 15:7-11	73
Deut 16:16b-17	76
Deut 20:19	86
Deut 24:19-22	73
Judges 2:21-22	42
Judges 11:39	24
1Sam 13:19-20	88
1Ki 4:5-7	72
1Ki 4:6	72
2Ki 19:23	91
Ezra 7:26	63
Job 12:7-10	89
Job 31:4	83
Job 34:21	83
Job 35:11	80
Job 37:23	88
Ps 8:1,3-6,9	80
Ps 9:11	38
Ps 10:4-6	84
Ps 14:1b-3	61
Ps 24:1	75
Ps 36:2	61
Ps 57:10	38
Ps 66:8	38
Ps 67:1-8	38
Ps 72:1-2	67
Ps 72:11-12	67
Ps 82:5	89
Ps 86:9	38
Ps 96:3	38
Ps 102:23	38
Ps 105:1	38
Ps 111:10	90
Ps 117:1	38
Ps 149:1	36
Ps 108:3	38
Prov 6:9-10	85
Prov 14:12	83
Prov 16:9	83, 91
Prov 20:26	63
Prov 21:1	60
Prov 28:28	60
Prov 29:4	62
Eccl 3:11	42
Is 24:5-6	85
Is 37:24	86
Is 40:6b	82
Is 44:9-13	83
Is 51:4	38
Is 52:1a	37
Jer 4:22a	86
Jer 4:23	86
Jer 4:25-26a	86
Jer 7:1-7	65
Jer 12:10.13	87
Jer 29:7	65, 77
Ez 26:19-20	87
Dan 2:21	60
Dan 5:12a	90
Hos 4:1-3	84, 86
Am 6:3.4.6	88
Am 8:4-6	75
Mal 3:10	76

Scripture References – New Testament

Mt 5:16	28, 49
Mt 5:20	50
Mt 5:32	30
Mt 5:39	47
Mt 6:19-24	74
Mt 6:25-34	26
Mt 7:12	50
Mt 19:6	29, 30
Mt 19:9	30

Mt 22:18-21 61
Mt 22:21b 66
Mt 22:37 79
Mt 22:37-39 43
Mt 25:14-30 73
Mt 25:23 35
Mt 25:35-36 77
Mt 25:40 33
Mt 28:18-20 38
Mt 28:19-20 .... 68, 77

Mk 4:26-32 49
Mk 7:20-21 83
Mk 12:30-31 33
Mk 16:15 .... 48, 93

Lk 6:29 47
Lk 12:15 85
Lk 12:42 72
Lk 14:31-33 26
Lk 16:2-4 72

Jn 1:14 89
Jn 2:1-11 27
Jn 2:6 24
Jn 3:16 46
Jn 3:16-17 25
Jn 6:44 49
Jn 6:65 49
Jn 14:13 53
Jn 16:13 92
Jn 16:23-26 52
Jn 17:14-16 66
Jn 19:10-11 60

Acts 2:8-11 39
Acts 2:38 90
Acts 4:12 .... 45, 46
Acts 5:29 62
Acts 14:16-17 44
Acts 16:1-3 32
Acts 17:11 56
Acts 17:22-23 43
Acts 17:26 38
Acts 17:27-28 89

Rom 1:19-20 .... 44, 89
Rom 2:14-16 43
Rom 3:9-10 64
Rom 3:10 46
Rom 3:20 25

Rom 3:22-26 25
Rom 3:23 22
Rom 3:23-24 61
Rom 7:19 83
Rom 8:19 93
Rom 8:28 82
Rom 11:36 76
Rom 12:2....23, 66, 89, 90
Rom 12:11 ....68, 77
Rom 13:1 60
Rom 13:1-2 61
Rom 13:4 60
Rom 13:5 61
Rom 13:13-14 ....36, 67
Rom 14:7-9 26
Rom 14:17 49
Rom 15:1 93
Rom 15:9-12 38

1Cor 2:15 90
1Cor 4:1-2 72
1Cor 5:12-13 46
1Cor 6:10 36
1Cor 6:12 27
1Cor 7:2 30
1Cor 7:12-16 51
1Cor 7:19 32
1Cor 8:9 37
1Cor 9:17 72
1Cor 9:19-23 50
1Cor 9:20-23 38
1Cor 10:20 44
1Cor 10:23 90
1Cor 10:26 75
1Cor 10:31 75
1Cor 12:1-31 41
1Cor 12:12-14 53

2Cor 1:19-20 92
2Cor 3:17 93
2Cor 5:19 89
2Cor 6:14-16 51

Gal 3:16-18 31
Gal 5:1 27
Gal 5:1-12 31
Gal 5:2b-3 32
Gal 5:13 27
Gal 6:2 76

Eph 3:2 72

Eph 4:14-15 54
Eph 4:17-18 83
Eph 4:19 87
Eph 4:23 90
Eph 5:3.5 87
Eph 5:10 22
Eph 5:22-25 29

Phil 2:10 44
Phil 2:10-11 .... 44, 45
Phil 2:15 49

Col 1:25 72
Col 2:8 84
Col 2:11-12a 32
Col 3:10 28
Col 3:11 .... 32, 39
Col 3:17 79

1Thess 4:12a 36
1Thess 5:21 .... 22, 56

1Tim 1:7 63
1Tim 2:1-2 65
1Tim 2:9a..................... 37
1Tim 4:12b 49
1Tim 6:10 75

2Tim 1:7 91
2Tim 2:24-25a 91

Tit 1:7 72

Hebr 1:1-2 44
Hebr 10:25 .... 33, 68, 77

1Petr 2:12 49
1Petr 2:13-14 61
1Petr 2:15 49
1Petr 3:9 48
1Petr 3:16 49
1Petr 4:10 72

1Jn 2:2 66
1Jn 4:1 22
1Jn 5:19 22
1Jn 5:21 23

2Jn 1:7-11 54

Rev 7:9-10 39

Index

References to Heidelberg Catechism

Question no. 1 .... 26, 75, 83
Question no. 3 25
Question no. 5 25
Question no. 6 .... 25, 74, 80
Question no. 7 .... 22, 83
Question no. 8 .... 46, 61
Question no. 9 64
Question no. 13 83
Question no. 13-14 .... 25, 46
Question no. 19 89
Question no. 20 46
Question no. 26-28 .... 26, 91
Question no. 27 83
Question no. 28 83
Question no. 34 27
Question no. 45 .... 28, 66, 90

Question no. 55 93
Question no. 60-64 46
Question no. 65 48
Question no. 68 29
Question no. 74 32
Question no. 86 .... 28, 90
Question no. 89 66
Question no. 91 27
Question no. 94-95 23
Question no. 103 33
Question no. 105 60
Question no. 108-109 30
Question no. 110 .... 36, 60, 75
Question no. 111 .... 33, 76
Question no. 117-120 53

www.ingramcontent.com/pod-product-compliance
Lightning Source LLC
Chambersburg PA
CBHW070516090426
42735CB00012B/2805